Loving Every Minute

52 Ways to Live,
Love & Laugh As A Woman

Dr. Judith Rolfs

Copyright 2016
Dr. Judith Rolfs

Dedication and Acknowledgements

To Mildred Rolfs and Bernice Vandy, my mother in-law and my mom who knew the importance of family and left a legacy of love I'm privileged to pass on. Special thanks to my publisher and editors at Kregel who published this book in print form as *A Woman's Guide: 52 Ways To Choose Happiness & Fulfillment* and have allowed me to distribute it.

I deeply appreciate the wisdom I acquired from countless women I counseled over the years many of whom I'm privileged to call friends. The insights from godly women who mentored me were invaluable. Lastly, my husband encouraged me to stay the course to get these ideas into a concise format to share. We're partners in every sense of the word – I treasure his humor and loving support.

What Readers Say About
Loving Every Minute:

"Judith Rolfs understands the challenges of being a Christian woman in a secular society and balancing roles in the home and workplace."

"Dr. Judith Rolfs' experiences as a Christian counselor, wife and mother provide a trustworthy perspective for the challenges and opportunities of single and married women as wives, and mothers."

"Judith helps women find creative ways to deepen their spiritual lives and honor their responsibilities to God, themselves, and others."

"A unique resource for women to use in personal Biblical devotions or group study!"

"The content in *Loving Every Minute* changed the way I relate to my husband my children, and even myself."

"Love, love this! I carry it as an e-book on my phone for instant inspiration."

"Dr. Rolfs' extensive counseling background provides invaluable insights for my everyday issues. She shares so openly and honestly! I'm not intimidated, but encouraged as I implement her suggestions."

Table of Contents

Introduction

Women, you are so precious to God, yet culture has many of you running at an unbelievable pace through the maze of daily life. Having often been a "runner" myself, I know how easy it is to become numb to the deeper realities of spiritual and emotional life. When excessive busyness sets in, you miss sharing what's truly important with your husband and children.

I went to graduate school to become an expert at helping families and found academic training alone didn't equip me for the job. I needed to apply the principles of Scripture and rely on the grace of God to help change lives. You'll find here the most useful principles I acquired from several decades of counseling women and families. I'm still in process, but I know what's in here works. My counseling clients who applied these 52 ways have seen the benefits.

I long to help you as well. I've recorded the 52 principles for you - plain and practical and fun to apply. I'm guessing as a Christian woman you made a decision when you asked Christ to be Lord of your life — to love Him and serve Him. As a married woman, you promised to love and be faithful to your husband all your life. When you first held your tiny baby, you committed yourself to love and protect this new life. But there's so much to learn and so many challenges every day. These "52 Ways" in *Loving Every Minute* can help you.

Some day I hope we can meet and celebrate victorious runs through life.

"Write the vision and make it plain on the tablets, that (s)he may run who reads it."

— Habakkuk 2:2

2

Ordering Your World

My friend Kathy keeps a giveaway bag in her closet for possessions her family no longer needs. Kathy also has a clutter bag on her kitchen counter for emotional garbage she needs to discard. This reminds her every day to keep throwing away inappropriate feelings of jealousy, anger, desire for revenge toward people who've hurt her, disappointments, and so on. She's a sweet, godly lady because she doesn't let her "junk" get out of order.

Clutter is the opposite of order. To clutter means to litter or pile in a disordered state. Clutter isn't just an accumulation of papers and odd socks - it can also be an accumulation of thoughts, ideas, and emotional feelings. Emotional clutter is bad because it chokes and kills order and beauty. We want to keep your heads, hearts, and hands clutter-free.

Disordered emotional feelings and thoughts make it harder to maintain physical order. Did you ever notice how hard it is to keep your home organized when you're emotionally upset? Or how living in physical disorder all around you makes it harder to keep thoughts and feelings orderly? Clutter creates a vicious cycle.

If clutter and disorder have taken over your home or your life, how do you start the clean up? You can examine with a ruthless eye whatever needs reordering and then eliminate anything that's not 1) essential, 2) healthy, 3) productive, or 4) fun.

Let's start with feelings. What makes you collect more possessions than you need or can use? Insecurity? Anger at a husband who doesn't meet your needs? Do you punish him by running up your charge cards? Do you live in fear of a future shortfall? Identify and throw this emotional garbage away.

Maybe you're caught in a chain of inherited physical clutter — too much junk! Perhaps your mom was a collector and now so are you. All that stuff must be sorted through and the excess removed regularly. Should you save the last inch of paint because you might need it someday? If you do need it again, chances are you won't be able to find it or it'll have dried up. Can't God provide paint again? Wouldn't He prefer to help you find the right paint than have you accumulate "stuff"? How do you decide what to keep. Ask two questions: Is it necessary? Does it spark joy when I see it?

Perhaps the words "waste not, want not" were drummed into you. They aren't in the Bible, you know. "Give, and it will be given to you" is written in God's Word (Luke 6:38). Sometimes things aren't in order because you haven't decided where to put them, or you think order requires too much work. Actually, order saves more time and makes life easier.

How about activities? Is your daily life too cluttered? Are there a thousand good things you could do each day, many work opportunities, all kinds of choices for the way you and your family spend your time? Ask God for wisdom in choosing what's best. Draw up a plan. Every household I've ever visited runs better when the members follow a routine that sets the structure for each day, each week, and each month.

How many new schedules or new routines for organization have you started only to have each fall by the wayside within a week or two, maybe even days or hours? Your reordered schedule needs to be flexible, fun, and beneficial in order to give you the motivation to stick to it.

Remember, moms, you are usually the hub of the scheduling activity that goes on in a household. One of my client's favorite phrases was "I've got to get my family on a good schedule," as if a plan is a living creation that could manage her household for her. One of my clients tried dozens of schedules before she came to me. She'd go through a period of discouragement and then start the cycle again: new plan, start, stop, new plan, start, stop.

My suggestion to her was keep life simple. Plan in terms of priorities: God, family, work, friends. Based on these four areas, evaluate your schedule three times a year during the major change times of your family life:

1. At the start of the school year
2. In January when school starts up after Christmas
3. In June when school lets out

If you're single or married without children, evaluate September 1, January 1, and June 1. Consider mealtime, bedtime, chore expectations, and general life changes. For example, yard cleanup goes on the June chart, snow removal on the January chart. Have at least one meal a day as a family — breakfast or dinner. Decide with your husband how strictly you want to enforce your rules. Explain your decision to your children and remind them often of the consequences of disobedience.

Start children off with a morning prayer you pray together: "God, please order our thoughts, our activities, and our things. Bless and protect us and bless others through us."

Tell a close friend about your decision to keep every area in your life — including your schedule — free from clutter. Have a "clutter accountability check" with someone once a week.

📖 Exploring Scripture

Read Genesis 1:4-10. Notice how God divided light from darkness and then labeled what He did. How's that for organization?

Next God took time to review His work and "saw that it was good." Taking time to feel satisfaction from what you've accomplished stimulates you to continue projects.

📖 Taking Action

- Make a list of the areas in your home and in your emotions that need to be "uncluttered."

- What activities can you eliminate from your schedule?

Prayer

Lord, reveal any disorder in my life that has come from thoughts and feelings like envy, bitterness, or guilt. Please help me remove the clutter of too many possessions and too many activities.

Representing Christ

C hances are if people don't relate to a sales rep, they won't want to do business. In the same way in your various roles, you represent Jesus Christ to the people you meet. If they don't like what they see in you, they may write Christ off their list.

I often observe our daughters and daughter-in-law in their roles as representatives of Christ. Along with her primary job of mothering, Tamara is a behind-the-scenes business consultant in her husband's computer software company. She's also an avid tennis player. Wherever she goes, Tamara works to promote family values in her Christian and non-Christian environments.

Pamela, a former math teacher, home-schools her three children. She participates in church and community activities.

Kathy is the assistant to the president of a major magazine and helps her husband juggle his career in computer and electronics with doctoral studies at the university. By her example she witnesses with sensitivity and discretion in both her business and social worlds. These are wonderful women aware of their roles. They desire to represent Christ in everything they do.

First and foremost in our lives, nothing must ever come before Jesus. Husband, job, home, church — we can't allow anything to become a bigger passion in life than Jesus. Our purpose needs to be clear to both ourselves and others. We must keep our primary purpose!

Second, Christ values our womanhood and our work. Our talk and our behavior show others that we are aware of our dignity and value the roles that we play.

Third, get into the light. Being a Christian doesn't mean you are to keep a low profile and stay in the background. "I'm not capable." "It's too much hassle." "What good could it do anyway?" are common excuses for avoiding using our authority as God's rep. God empowers what He inspires. Don't be afraid to bring up spiritual issues.

Fourth, be diligent and leave the results to Him. Be like the housewife who took on the challenge of making some important changes in the public school her children attend or the young female lawyer who took on a team of seasoned defense lawyers with perseverance and diligence because she knew her cause was right.

Lastly, pray and let Christ decide where you are to work as His representatives always bathing your activities in prayer.

📕 *Exploring Scripture*

You can be a representative of Christ because you've received authority and empowerment. Matthew 28:18-20. "All authority has been given to Me in heaven and on earth. Go therefore [because of it] and make disciples of all the nations, baptizing them in the name of the Father and of the Son and of the Holy Spirit, teaching them to observe all things that I have commanded you; and lo, I am with you always, even to the end of the age."

These words of Scriptures inspire and encourage me. Put simply, God's message is, "I'm giving you everything you need to represent me and encourage people to live by my teachings. I'll help you do it and never leave you alone."

Romans Chapter 16 illustrates the powerful role of women in the early church with its wonderful descriptions of female representatives of our Lord. Romans 16:1-2 reads, "I commend to you Phoebe our sister, who is a servant of the church in Cenchrea, that you may receive her in the Lord in a manner worthy of the saints, and assist her in whatever business she has need of you; for indeed she has been a helper of many and of myself also." These early examples recorded in letters of the apostles give us ongoing instruction how the church should operate today.

In Verse 4, "[Priscilla and Aquila] risked their own necks for my life, to whom not only I give thanks, but also all the churches of the Gentiles." Verse 6 says, "Greet Mary, who labored much for us." At least seven women are referred to in this chapter. Whenever someone says they'd like to represent Christ in society but they don't like the subservient role of Christian women, show them Romans 16 for starters.

📖 *Taking Action*

- Does your talk and your behavior show others that you're aware of your dignity and value?

- How can you better project yourself in order to attract others to the Lord?

- Take a moment to write down your various roles.

- Are you humbly accepting your roles?

- What good can you accomplish in your environments as God's representative?

- What, if anything, keeps you from exercising your role as God's representative in the world?

Prayer

Lord, reveal to me through Your Word where and how I can best represent You in my roles as a wife, mom, daughter, friend, volunteer, sister, employer/e, neighbor.

Deepening Friendships

J esus had intense social contacts with people. He often bypassed surface-level conversation With the Samaritan woman at the well in John 4, He got right to the heart of what mattered to her —her marital relationships.

What had she been seeking that was lacking in her life? Jesus knew it was Himself, the Living Water. Her thirsting was related to unquenched desires that nothing on earth could fulfill, and He told her so.

I imagine the woman at the well was surprised at Jesus' talk. He spoke to her and actually looked at her. How many people had passed this woman by, even shunned her over the years? Jesus knew all about her past. He cared about her and what was in her best interests now.

Jesus and the woman at the well became friends right then and there. For sure. Then she wanted to share Him — the way we all like to introduce friends to one another — "This is someone I think is special; you will, too, as soon as you get to know each other."

Jesus is a great friend and master communicator. I teach counseling clients the four different levels of communication. Knowing these can improve your ability to form deep friendships and relate to others. Here are examples of each.

- Level One — Cliché Conversation. "How are you?" "Fine." (There's no real honesty like, "I'm having a bad day" or "I feel great because...")

- Level Two — Reporting Facts.
  "I have a cold."
  "It's raining hard."

- Level Three — Ideas or Judgments.
  "Everybody should take vitamins."
  "It's lucky I brought my umbrella."

- Level Four — Feelings or Emotions.
  "I'm disappointed I can't go skiing."
  "The rain always makes me feel a little down."

An effective communicator must be willing to reveal herself, talk about her failings, and discuss personal things. She cries when she's moved, and she can laugh at herself and others. She can tease, and she tempers her serious comments with levity.

Her listener(s) feel like she's interacting with them at Level Four. My daughter Pam has become close friends with the woman who delivers her mail by taking the time to chat and asking how her day is going, just as Jesus asked the woman at the well and then listened with caring.

My friend Pat is a "Level Four" friend. She always wants to know how people really are. In turn she tells her dreams and dilemmas. She shares her deepest self in a thousand ways. Because our communication is intimate, Pat knows when I have a physical or emotional or spiritual need, and is eager to help.

When we moved to a large house twenty years ago, Pat found extra furniture for us. We still use the kitchen table! When we went to Europe recently, she and her husband, Tom, veteran travelers, outlined an agenda for us. When our son was hospitalized in another city, Pat came to spend a few days and pray with me. When our daughter Pam married, Pat and her daughter Caryl made the bridesmaids' bouquets and decorated the church. I am incredibly blessed by the wonderful friends God has put into my life.

Meaningful friendships develop by going past communication Levels One, Two and Three. This doesn't mean you share your deepest feelings with every person we meet. Like Jesus we must pray for the Father's wisdom to be discerning. But it's important to be open to Level Four communication. Keep striving for deep, honest conversations.

📖 *Exploring Scripture*

What you say and how you say it affects your friendships. What can you learn from these Scriptures?

- Proverbs 27:2 — "Let another man praise you, not your own mouth."

- Ecclesiastes 5:3b — "And a fool's voice is known by his many words."

- Ephesians 4:29 — "Do not let any unwholesome talk come out of your mouths, but only what is helpful for building others up according to other needs, that it may benefit those who listen." (NIV).

📖 *Taking Action*

Are there some women in your life you'd like as closer friends? Write their names here.

Arrange to meet these women for lunch or coffee and practice developing your communication skills. It's OK to tell these friends you'd like to deepen your friendship with them and work on your relational skills. That's being open.

Prayer

Lord, lead me to the friends who will minister in my life and for whom I can be a true Christian sister.

Ditching Demons

*D*emons are often mentioned in the New Testament, but not talked about much today. Ever wonder where they've all gone? Have demons become extinct like dinosaurs? I wish! The existence of demons is real. Many women, including me, would prefer to forget about them, but that's not what Jesus did. He recognized the presence of demons and dealt with them.

Demons haven't stopped their powerful, destructive work. If you're having turmoil in your home, check if you've given an opportunity for the Devil to enter. Get rid of games, music, magazines, books, TV programs, ornaments, or decorations that could serve as doorways into your spirits or the spirit of any member of your family. You have full authority in the name of Jesus to calmly order demons to take off.

Ouija boards, horoscopes, occult-related computer games, music, and rituals may be experimented with at parties our children may attend. You need to discuss openly these spiritual dangers with them, just as you discuss physical safety. Anything connected with the occult or witchcraft is destructive and must be avoided.

I counseled a fourteen-year-old boy with green hair. He had a history of drug use in junior high school in Florida. He had come to Wisconsin from Florida to live with his grandmother in a Christian home. He said he wanted to get his act together and agreed to live by his grandmother's rules, but he violated them over and over. Each time he disobeyed he sounded genuinely sorry, but he'd soon repeat the offense.

During our counseling sessions, I discovered he'd brought his satanic rock music, pictures, and occult jewelry with him to his grandmother's house. I encouraged him to get rid of these connections to his satanic past and his rebellion stopped.

The fourth-grade daughter of a young mom I counseled ran away from home several times. The police found the girl each time, and she willingly returned. During counseling the mom revealed the girl had a computer game with witches and sorcerers in which the main character always died. The girl loved the game. One day, to the mother's amazement, the daughter shoved the computer game into her closet and said she hated it.

Almost immediately the girl's disposition changed dramatically for the better. Several days later, the daughter felt compelled to take the game out again. The mom didn't object. As soon as the girl began playing the game, her out-of-control behavior resumed. The mom refused to believe my suggestion that her daughter's behavior and the game were connected. She was afraid of her daughter's reaction if she got rid of the game permanently. The seesaw continued.

In counseling there are times when I identify a perverse, demonic resistance in a client who knows what to do to be free but refuses to comply.

Satan is a subtle, slippery spirit with weapons that can fool us. One of his most effective weapons is to toss accusations at you and fill you with self-doubt. Put-downs and mockery are his specialty. Ever hear anything like this: "You're too loud" or "too quiet" or "too pushy" or "not assertive enough" or "not qualified" or "not capable," "You sure messed up that situation, dummy," or "You shouldn't have gotten involved?"

Another wily trick to watch out for is a grumbling spirit. You can identify it when you talk to yourself in words like "I'm always left to handle all the details" or "Just once, I wish I didn't have to do this."

Warning! Guard against developing "demon mania" and dumping everything on demons. There are three sources of temptation: the world, the flesh, and the devil — not just demons. Don't look for a demon everywhere. C. S. Lewis sums up the right attitude toward evil spirits in his classic book, *The Screwtape Letters.* He claims the two biggest dangers regarding Satan are focusing on the devil too much and ignoring the devil's existence entirely - equally harmful. Learn the facts about these wily spirits.

📖 *Exploring Scripture*

- Mark 1:39: "And He was preaching in their synagogues throughout all Galilee, and casting out demons." Demons were and are quite common.

- Mark 5: 3-4: "This man lived in the tombs, and no one could bind him any more, not even with a chain. For he had often been chained hand and foot, but he tore the chains apart and broke the irons on his feet. No one was strong enough to subdue him" (NIV). Demons can incite amazing physical strength.

- Mark 5:5: "Night and day among the tombs and in the hills he would cry out and cut himself with stones" (NIV). Demons can urge people to cut themselves or otherwise harm their bodies.

- Mark 7:29-30: "Then He (Jesus) told her, 'For such a reply, you may go; the demon has left your daughter'" (NIV). Demons can enter children.

- Mark 5: 6-7: "When he saw Jesus from a distance, he ran and fell on his knees in front of him. He shouted at the top of his voice, 'What do you want with me, Jesus, Son of the Most High God? Swear to God that you won't torture me!'" (NIV). Demons recognize Jesus!

Demons may be present, but Jesus has given us control. If you come in contact with a demon, apply the Word of God in Luke 10:17b: "Lord, even the demons submit to us in your name" (NIV). Second Thessalonians 3:3 reads, "But the Lord is faithful, and he will strengthen and protect you from the evil one" (NIV).

📖 *Taking Action*

Take preventive measures. The technique for identifying counterfeit money is to study the real thing. Fill your own and your children's minds and hearts with the truth about Jesus and with wholesome activities, thoughts, words, and media experiences.

Jesus deals with demons forcefully. In Mark 5:12-13 we read, "The demons begged Jesus, 'Send us among the pigs; allow us to go into them'" (NIV). Notice when the unclean spirits entered the swine, the swine destroyed themselves. Demonic involvement can lead to human self-destruction.

Teach your children 1) the devil is real and 2) to resist him, and he will take off. Another way to give an "in" to the devil is through anger and discord with others. Ephesians

4:26-27 says, "Never go to bed angry — don't give the devil that sort of foothold" (PHILLIPS).

How can you apply these words daily?

Prayer

Lord, show me any foothold that Satan has in my life and home. Give me strength to resist Satan. Thank You for Your protection and for making Satan flee when I resist him.

FIVE
Exposing Myths

C hristian women always have their act together, never experience pain, and live problem-free lives. They are always kind and loving. They never dislike or judge others. Christian women are rarely discouraged, depressed, or confused. Christian women are perfect. Wrong! These are myths. Craving this false idea of perfection is dangerous.

Some women worry about being overly religious so they bury their Christianity so deep even their own neighbors don't know they're Christians. Others talk a lot about God, but not enough to Him.

Another myth is that all single men and all single women secretly yearn to be married. Not true. Some do, but many are quite content serving God in their singleness and do not desire what God didn't intend. Love is a commitment to service whether it's toward a mate, a child, a family or church member, or a stranger. Marriage is never an equal partnership. Both partners must work 100% to make the marriage work.

Believing one Christian denomination is the only way to Christ is another myth. That would mean only all Baptists or Methodists or whatever in heaven. No way! No one Christian style of practice based on solid, sound, scriptural doctrine is superior to another. Christ is the Way. The people in heaven will have come through Christ, and they will love the Lord their God with all their heart, soul, and strength, and their neighbor, too.

The problem with believing myths is that they rob you of joy. And the joy of the Lord is your strength to go on living rich and fulfilled each day. Life will always have problems. The kingdom of heaven may begin on earth, but it only starts here. This is the space between your pre-birth presence of God and your after death presence of God. Stop bemoaning the existence of problems and focus your energy on coping with life as it really is. The tough experiences of real life can lead to greater knowledge and love of our Lord.

Believing myths is dangerous! Some women withdraw from being involved in life at all. Do you ever wonder why young, lovely, intelligent women commit suicide? Or anorexic women starve themselves to death? Or women become obsessive-compulsive about their homes or their work? Belief in a myth — a lie — has gripped them, controls them, and they can no longer function normally. Sometimes they can no longer function at all.

On the journey of life we will never reach perfection, but we can exhibit healthy attitudes, practices, and relationships. Healthy, scriptural principles enable women to cope with real life and keep promises and commitments to God, self, families, and friends.

🖋 Exploring Scripture

Rahab (Joshua 2:1-21) wasn't perfect. Deborah (Judges 4:4-14) and Jael (Judges 4:17-22) weren't perfect either. Each was God's woman in God's time in God's place. Each gave Him her best. God made good come from each life, and He'll do the same for you.

📖 Taking Action

- I bundled many myths together here to get you thinking about yourself and your life. Make out your own list of the myths you believe. Discuss with a friend which ones you need to get rid of and why.

- Are there any areas where you're expecting perfection from yourself or others? You are human, after all, and Jesus loves you as you are. Prayerfully ask God what you need to do about unrealistic expectations. My prayer for you is that God will reveal constructive changes to you.

Prayer

Lord, it's so easy for myths and lies to slip into my thoughts and feelings. Keep me focused on Your Word and Your truth. Free me from believing myths. Each day may I grow more and more like You.

Staying Calm, Cheerful, and Consistent

*D*o you sometimes get caught up in the swirl and whirl of life? I do. It happens when I'm too rushed and I berate myself for trying to do too much in too short a time. I feel myself becoming tense.

When the game, the deal, the family problem is on the line, tension can become a vibrating sensation. It's time for the CCC Plan, which is always effective when you remember to use it. CCC stands for staying CALM, CHEERFUL, AND CONSISTENT.

When you choose to be calm and cheerful, consistent with your Christian beliefs, you don't say or do things you'll regret later. The circumstances don't change, but you can stay focused in your thoughts and actions, which makes all the difference! We keep operating in a straight line instead of functioning in circular fashion and ending up completely flustered and right back where we started.

The CCC Plan is especially important in disciplining children. A client used to have to be furious before she'd correct or spank her child. Then she'd lose control and start yelling. When she learned to stay calm, cheerful, and act consistently with her beliefs about children's proper behavior, the whole atmosphere of her home became more pleasant.

📖 Exploring Scripture

Is this all psychobabble? No, the principle is as old as the Bible. Jesus taught the CCC Plan, and He always modeled it. Take the storm on the Sea of Galilee when the frantic apostles awakened Jesus. He could have jumped up and said, "Oh no, what are we going to do now?" Jesus stayed cheerful and calm.

Jesus knew He could stop the storm, and remember He can stop your storm too. What a model of calmness, cheerfulness, and consistency we have in Jesus in John 1:14-22! Even in His anger when He cleansed the temple, He showed control and turned the act into a lesson for His disciples. Other incidents in the Gospels also reveal Jesus showing CCC.

📖 Taking Action

Here are tips for staying calm, cheerful, and consistent over the small stuff, which creates most of your emotional stress:

1. When you feel flustered, often your natural inclination is to rush ahead in your thoughts and movements. Instead, start to move and speak in slow motion. You can regain mastery by being CCC.

2. You can calm or cheer yourself in seconds when you pray. Focusing on Jesus and eternity can relax you. What you're doing at the moment takes on a different perspective.

3. Think about something pleasant, relaxing, or rewarding that you've done or are going to do — a cup of tea, where you're going next month, a cozy time to read a book.

4. Picture yourself acting calm, cheerful, and consistent. Acting "as if" truly helps your body focus on becoming what you portray. Act brave, graceful, and determined.

5. If cooperating with the inevitable is your only choice, do it with CCC like an heir of God.

CCC comes from knowing He has ultimate control. Preserve your emotional energy. You can't be casual about an overwhelming problem like a sick child or a company take-over that's threatening your job. But, even then, don't drain your precious emotional reserves with hysteria.

6. Meditate on the "peace" verses in Scripture.

- When are you most challenged to remain calm, cheerful, and consistent?
- Which of the suggested behaviors might work for you?
- Record how you'll apply them this week.

Prayer

Lord, thank You that I can come to You in prayer when my life becomes frenzied and chaotic. Thank You for modeling calm, cheerful, and consistent behavior in the storm. I want Your Spirit to fill me; I long to exhibit peace like You.

Decorating Your Temples

SEVEN

W omen have two temples to decorate — the personal temple of soul and body, occupied by the Holy Spirit, and the temple that is your home. I'll talk about your home in this section, and bodies and souls in "Keeping Body and Soul Fit" (16).

God created beauty on earth as recorded in Genesis. Later, when a temple, an earthly dwelling, was to be built for God, He gave directions about every minute detail making sure it was decorated according to His specifications. Picky, picky! Yes! So should you be in your innate desire to create a comfortable nest for yourself and your family.

Occasionally you may hear that a Christian shouldn't be interested in material possessions but it's okay to appreciate nice things. Man's first home was awesome, the Garden of Eden, and your future home is heaven. Enhance your surroundings is great as long as it's affordable and not detracting from the priority of God. There's nothing wrong with living in a visually pleasant, organized setting.

Notice I didn't say expensive. You can have a lovely home on a small budget. Often what a home needs more than anything else is simply a creative reorganization. (See Section 5, "Ordering Your World.")

Instead of adding more things, consider streamlining and giving space to your favorite possessions. Get creative with the furnishings you have with slipcovers. Design a new cozy sitting area in the living room or kitchen. Try angling your furniture diagonally across corners of the room.

Shopping for second-hand furniture is an inexpensive way to refurbish a house one item at a time.

I like an eclectic style and appreciate the design of older furniture so much of my furniture comes from second-hand shops. These pieces have character and interesting stories to tell, and the price is usually reasonable. Our daughter-in-law found a gorgeous floral chintz sofa at the Salvation Army for a fifth of its cost new.

I pray over anything I bring into our home — for the people who made it, for those who used it before me (if it's not new), and for my family to be blessed by our temporary ownership because everything we own is only ours for a time.

Check out magazines and catalogs at the library for ideas. A friend of mine makes stunning slipcovers and drapes from sheets. She uses hidden cup hooks and rubber bands to hang the drapes. With T-pins she holds the fabric in place on her furniture covers. Her creativity has turned into a thriving small business for her.

If you can do what needs doing yourself, you'll receive creative satisfaction as well as save money on your projects. Painting wood furniture or stripping, staining, and varnishing a painted piece is like getting a brand-new piece of furniture! Don't get carried away with a Do-It-Yourself project, though, if it creates emotional distress and frustration in you. D.I.Y. is not always cheaper or fun. Factor in your time as well as your talent.

If you're not gifted in this area, ask friends who are to help you redecorate or rearrange. How about a progressive closet cleaning? Share your resources and your talents. Ladies from a church I visited in Florida move from house to house and clean one person's closets per week, or they go to three or four homes in one day and clean one closet at each house. (Yes, this takes humility.)

Once a month a Baptist church offers a decorating day for anyone in the church who requests help. Women bring their sewing machines, donated curtains, glue, paintbrushes, hammers, and nails. The homemaker shares in advance where she would most like help. One room or perhaps the entire house may need to be redone. Everyone brings a bag lunch. The women visit as they work and enjoy making one another's homes more attractive.

Other group projects might include planting flower or vegetable gardens in spring and sharing perennials by thinning and dividing them. These "day-outs" are so much fun and also inexpensive. Many hands and heads work more efficiently.

A word of caution: Don't get too much ego tied into your house. That's dangerous. Fabrics and furniture wear; styles change. Jesus is the same yesterday, today, and forever, and makes all things new. He's the safest spot for every woman's ego.

🕮 *Exploring Scripture*

Read 2 Chronicles 3 to see how precisely the temple in Jerusalem was built and decorated. The temple was created according to God's exact specifications as precisely as humans could build because the building was an act of worship in itself. The temple was to be used for worshipers sacrificing offerings to God.

Everything about us can exalt God. He delights in having your home as lovely as possible— whether we live in a hut, a motor home, or an estate.

📖 *Taking Action*

- What homemaking talent do you have that you could share with the other women in your church?

- Look around your home with a critical eye. What does it need? More color, texture, design?

- Would a transformation with sheets, rubber bands, and T-pins help?

Prayer

Lord, I long to make the temple I dwell in as attractive as possible. Help me to use things I own to their best advantage and be gracious in accepting positive suggestions of my friends. May I be generous in helping others as well.

EIGHT

Growing in Love

A strong, lasting marriage is pleasing to God. The Knotts, a prominent political couple who lived in Tallahassee, Florida, were married over seventy years. They died within eight days of each other. He was 101; she was 93. After all those years, they couldn't be separated more than a week!

A friend of mine describes her marriage, "After thirty years my husband and I almost don't need words to communicate. He knows what I'm thinking and I know what he's thinking. We still talk, because we like the sound of each other's voice. But," she adds, "the first ten years of our marriage I would have traded in my husband in many times if my circumstances would have allowed it. Now I can't imagine life without him."

Looking back I, too, consider it a miracle of God's grace that my husband and I survived the first seven years of marriage. I wanted to have the perfect marriage. This desire was a great cause of confusion and discord. We were two strong-willed, independent people accustomed to pleasing ourselves. We were in for an adjustment shock and at times great pain.

The second week of marriage we had a horrible argument over my husband's socks — I had misplaced some in the wash and became as defensive as a bull when he demanded I be more careful. I didn't sleep all night, sure that I'd married a hypercritical tyrant — definitely the wrong man. Over those first months I often asked God if our union was a mistake.

I admit now I wasn't Mrs. Perfection, but then I didn't realize how many faults I had. We had more downs than ups as God made my husband and me wiser in Him and created strong and beautiful bonds despite our inadequacies. What a thrill to experience God's changes!

Occasionally I stepped in and did things that I should have let my husband do. Desiring to please and help a husband is an ingrained characteristic. Problems increased when my husband took advantage of my helpful nature. It took many years to work out the right balance in our work, parenting, and ministry.

It's true at times my husband still frustrates me, and I annoy him when we both see a situation from totally different perspectives. Now we laugh. We've been married over fifty years, and he still does things that are incomprehensible to me. But most often, miraculously, we are like-minded.

Many of the women I counseled wondered about their choice of mate at some time or other. I've observed most people tend to marry someone like-minded in values but different in personality. They agree about most things, but not about everything. (There can be no interrelationship between two entities that are identical.) But when the differences of temperament pop out between two people, they seem to overshadow the similarities.

Do you ever feel like bailing out? Remember, this isn't a seven-year contract you promised. Marriage is for a lifetime of mutual change for the better. You were created by God to be a helpmate.

A smooth marital relationship is easier, of course, if you married a Christian man or a man with personal integrity. Maybe you didn't. It's easy to lose your respect for your husband if he acts unethically. However, God doesn't lose respect for your husband's personhood. God appreciates your husband even when He sees behavior He dislikes. God remains committed and expects you to do the same.

📕 *Exploring Scripture*

Song of Songs 8:6-7 describes what real love for your spouse: "Place me like a seal over your heart, like a seal on your arm; for love is as strong as death, its jealousy unyielding as the grave. It burns like blazing fire, like a mighty flame. Many waters cannot quench love; rivers cannot wash it away. If one were to give all the wealth of his house for love, it would be utterly scorned." (NIV).

- Love can be genuine or superficial. What kind of love is Solomon describing here?

- Read Psalm 26, "The Prayer of a Good Man," and pray this psalm may be true for your husband.

📖 *Taking Action*

- My "3-3 Tip" — What is there to appreciate about your spouse right now? Make a list of three things you appreciate about him, tell him what they are, and remind yourself of them three times a day.

- The most powerful (and often overlooked) way you can be a helper is to pray for your husband. A man can be protected from temptations if he has a wife who prays for him. Write down three specific areas you will pray about. Pray for thirty days and see what happens.

Prayer

Lord, give my husband wisdom in every decision, big and little. Help him grow in character qualities pleasing to You, Lord. Use him directly or indirectly to further Your kingdom. Shelter him from any harm — physical, emotional, or spiritual.

Respecting Your Mate

*D*uring counseling sessions I often hear women use put-downs about her husband's shortcomings. I can only guess how they must talk at home!

If somebody nags us or yells, we feel demeaned, disrespected, and put down, and so do our husbands! God never yells or nags. Remember when you speak to your husband it can take a long time to restore emotional intimacy after you've yelled or made sarcastic or callous comments to your mate. Make a point to never dump your crabbiness or disappointment on your husband. You maintain the passion in your marriage with tender words, kindness, and loving, physical intimacy.

Over the years through my counseling experiences I've collected ten ideas about respecting and loving husbands.

Ten Ways to Show Respect and Love for Your Husband That Can Keep You Out of Counseling:

1. Give up the bad memories. If for whatever reason you're harboring resentment, ask God to enable you to drop it. Harboring resentment makes you overly sensitive and subtly hostile.

2. Be polite at all times. A Hungarian woman married fifty years claims there's seldom been a harsh word between her and her husband. Unrealistic? A friend said, "You don't really believe that!" I do. I believe this takes a lot of effort, but it's worth it!

3. Avoid complaining — subtly implied or spoken aloud. Spouses have sensitive antennas. No sniping, sarcasm, name-calling, or other rudeness. And never tell your children negative things about their father!

4. Blend your interests with your husband's so that you can have time together. If he loves to fish and you don't, maybe you'd enjoy sitting in the boat reading. Do more of what brings you closer and less of what doesn't.

5. Make time for love. Most sexual problems arise from being too busy or too tired. Overscheduling your life makes it hard to keep special dates for lovemaking. By the way there's nothing wrong with love appointments — you enjoyed dates when you courted!

6. Be militant about having a good relationship and not letting anyone or anything interfere with it — not even parents, in-laws, children, brothers, sisters. Show your husband you respect his opinions, feelings, and desires. Expect some bumps, but be solution oriented when there's a difficulty.

7. Surprise him. Do the unexpected. Try a kiss instead of a grumble, even if you're in a situation where grumbling seems right. You'll find you get what you give. He may start surprising you.

8. Stay away from people who help feed negativity about your spouse. Share any problem very discreetly outside the relationship. Avoid "spouse attack."

9. Remember divorce doesn't solve the problems you think it will; it creates different ones and hurts children whatever their age. Find causes and explanations for your husband's behavior. See him as a unique individual and listen to his point of view.

10. Your husband chose you and you him. Be loyal to the commitment you made. Shine the light on yourself and find ways you can both grow into a mature couple.

📕 Exploring Scripture

Here are several Scriptures that are powerhouse verses for relationships:

- "A gentle answer turns away wrath" (Proverbs 15:1 NIV).

- "Refrain from anger and turn from wrath; do not fret — it leads only to evil" (Psalm 37:8 NIV).

📖 Taking Action

- Praise your husband in front of your child or children. Make him a "Great Husband" or "Father of the Year" certificate and hang it on the refrigerator where everyone will see it.

- Ask him what you can do to improve your relationship with him. Write it down and remember to do it each week.

- Think of any ways you tend to "put down" your husband. What positive terms can you use to replace negative comments?

Prayer

Lord, please help me to see the good things about my husband and to remember to praise him for those qualities. Increase my loyalty and help me to choose friends who will help and not hurt my marriage. Quiet my complaining spirit. May I surprise my husband with love.

TEN

Trusting God

When you're really down or going through an incredibly tough time, can you believe God is at work, even in the mess or devastation you see?

Greg and Gail's nine-year-old daughter was killed in a car accident months after the girl had received Christ and brought her entire family to the Lord. Gail's prayer, the day after the accident, was that somehow God would use this terrible tragedy for good. She wrote a letter to pass out at her daughter's funeral, which was also published in the local paper, describing how her daughter had led the family to Christ and how she knew her daughter was in heaven with Jesus.

Still, the loss was almost more than their family could bear. It was the darkest, most difficult period of their lives. The hole left by their daughter's death will fill a little over the years, but it will never fill completely because a child is always part of the family. Gail and Greg are praying now about how to direct their extra time and energy.

The accident that claimed her daughter's life was out of anyone's control, and Gail realized it wasn't right to blame God for what happened. In other situations, however, I've observed that clients struggle to trust God because deep down in their hearts, they do blame Him. They believe an all-powerful God should be able to divert any difficulty.

Marietta, a single mom with two boys aged ten and seven, admits (although reluctantly) that maybe she did divorce her husband too hastily and for selfish reasons. Now he's remarried and has more children. She's struggling financially to raise her sons. As Marietta leans on God, she's discovering He will help her through these times even though she brought her afflictions and difficulties upon herself.

Fortunately, God's love and mercy do not depend on never making mistakes. Never despair when for a time things seem to get worse instead of better. Remember Creation and the culminating work of the cross at Calvary occurred during visible darkness. Never, ever, does God ignore your cries for help, no matter how dark your circumstances appear.

✒ *Exploring Scripture*

Going through a time when trusting God is difficult? Meditate on God's Word. "Shout for joy, O heavens; rejoice, O earth; burst into song, O mountains! For the LORD comforts his people and will have compassion on his afflicted ones" (Isaiah 49:13 NIV).

You can trust God when someone you love is sick emotionally or physically. "O LORD my God, I called to you for help and you healed me. O LORD, you brought me up from the grave; you spared me from going down into the pit." (Psalm 30:2 NIV). Sometimes someone you love is healed and changes and you have a wonderful, fruitful extended life for years. Perhaps your beloved is an addict or an abuser. You can still trust in God's care for you.

King David grieved for his son. He fasted and prayed and wouldn't stop while his ill son's life was in danger. But as soon as his son died, David got up and went about his business. Did King David still carry grief and sorrow for his son no longer with him? Of course. But King David knew his role as an intercessor was over and that God would want David to get on with God's purpose for King David's own life.

📖 *Taking Action*

- Who or what are your sources of security?

- Are they trustworthy?

- What do you need to trust God with right now?

Prayer

Dear Lord, help me to trust You through all the hard times of life — the things I do not understand and the hard things I think I could have prevented. Help me to put the past behind, growing in Your love and seeking Your purposes for me and my loved ones day by day.

ELEVEN

Praying Well

C an we become holy without talking with God and listening to His instructions? Can we become scuba divers without showing up for lessons? Hardly! The presence of God is the milieu, the environment in which your holiness is created and developed. That's how the holy people in the Bible got wisdom and drew close to God — by conversing with Him.

Over years of seeing God work repeatedly in response to her prayers, a friend of mine now says about everything, "I've got to pray about this." Whether it's a realtor wanting to list her house or it's deciding where to go for a vacation, she's developed the habit of asking God His plans for her before she does anything.

Beth knows she should pray more, and she means to. When she tries, it's sort of vague. She wonders when, why, and how to do it. Another friend, who has a job in a challenging nursing home setting, asks God to ordain her hands and her steps every time she enters the building. She prays, "May I give out the right medications to each of my patients and perform my many nursing tasks correctly."

You can pray about anything! My prayer for the garden in the woods around our house is that it resembles just a tiny bit of the Garden of Eden where God is honored with no disobedience. A peculiar thing to pray, but why not?

What is prayer anyway? Prayer is the link in the God-us relationship. Relationships require conversation and connection. Some people like to talk to God out loud when they go for a walk or talk to God when they're driving in the car.

Who should we pray for? All those in our family and our circle of friends, as well as the people we meet as we move through the day. While I wait in checkout lines at stores, I often pray for the clerk or the person next to me in line.

How should we pray? How about Paul's prayer: "For this reason we also, since the day we heard it, do not cease to pray for you, and to ask that you may be filled with the knowledge of His will in all wisdom and spiritual understanding; that you may walk worthy of the Lord, fully pleasing Him, being fruitful in every good work and increasing in the knowledge of God." (Colossians 1:9-10).

If you want to learn how to pray well, you need to study people like Hannah, a childless woman in the Old Testament. She made a desperate plea for a child and surrendered her life to God (1 Samuel 1:10). Esther is another great example of a woman who knew the value of prayer. She asked others to fast and pray for her before she approached the King (Esther 4:16).

What should we pray for? Hezekiah made a request for an extended life and God honored it.

There's nothing wrong with asking for specific needs.

Prayer is not a speech contest. David said simply and sincerely what was on his heart. He didn't edit himself to try to say nice things. He told God when he was frantic, joyful, fearful, angry. Paul's communication with God was slightly different. He threaded his words with praise.

Your words simply need to be genuine and sincere. Short prayers are OK. A short prayer forces you to focus in on the main message. Short and specific is great and so is long and detailed.

When should you pray? Always, all days. Prayer is the intimate whispering of your heart and listening for God's intimate answer. Today I prayed before I cleaned my closet, "Lord help me get rid of clothes I don't need and simplify my wardrobe." Then I went in and held up each item of clothing one by one and prayed, "Do you want to see me in this, Lord, yes or no? Is there someone I should give this to?" While I was doing this sorting, I looked at my watch and saw it was ten o'clock, and a young girl had asked me to pray for her test today. "Keep her calm, please, Lord, give her wisdom," I prayed.

How often do you need to bring your own family's needs to God? Daily. You send your children out with coats and mittens in the winter, rainwear in the spring, and sunscreen in the summer to protect them physically. Don't forget their spiritual and emotional protection. You can pray, "Lord, please send ministering angels to surround, guide and protect my child today. Thank You for hearing my prayer."

📖 *Exploring Scripture*

"Then He spoke a parable to them, that men always ought to pray and not lose heart." (Luke 18:1). Jesus told about the widow who kept after a judge to help her get justice until the judge finally agreed to help. You can't expect instant answers as if God is a divine drive-through. But the minute you pray, you release supernatural power into a situation and you'll eventually see the fruits of your prayers.

40

📖 Taking Action

There's nothing more powerful you can do for those you love than regularly pray for them. Will you make a commitment to be a daily prayer warrior for the needs of others God puts into your life? Start a prayer notebook now. List people and their needs. Next to each name write a short sentence about specifically what you're asking God to do in their lives right now.

List the people who need prayer and the situations you need to pray about.

Prayer

Lord, I need to pray continually; I need to bathe my very life in prayer. Help me to think first to pray, linking You into every thought and event and person of my life. Thank You that You hear every prayer and love and answer.

TWELVE

Playing Like a Child

The beauty of having children and grandchildren is that you get to experience again what a child sees, thinks and feels. You get to enjoy things like watching water flow from a faucet turn or feeling a breeze blow, smelling grass freshly washed by rain, and feeling soap slip through your fingers. All the ordinary things become extraordinary when you stop to appreciate them like a child.

When you use all of your senses to touch, taste, smell, hear, see everything around you, you feel the wings of a butterfly or the smoothness of a pen or capture the scent of evergreen needles in a little box remembering Christmas in March. You give yourself the gift of wondering and pretending with your children. You get to experience these joys with them, and for a moment set aside training, directing and simply enjoy life with children.

Why did Jesus want the little children to come near Him? He delighted in their presence as we should. Children are wise in many ways. They savor experiences rather than speeding through them. Children who haven't been overscheduled in too many activities move with a smooth innate rhythm. I've learned so much from my children and grandchildren.

My friend Jane's children grew up around her like unappreciated wildflowers. Jane never took time to laugh and play with her children. One day she heard a lecture on humor and realized there wasn't enough laughter in her family's life. She decided to try telling silly stories and developing private jokes to share with each of her children. Her children had never heard her laughing except at the movies. Although her children were adolescents by then, they loved her efforts. Jane was amazed at the warmth and joy that humor added to her family's life. Such a simple thing, but Jane had never tried it before.

📖 *Exploring Scripture*

I imagine Jesus and His disciples shared great fun and private jokes. In Psalm 126:2 we read about laughter, "Then our mouth was filled with laughter, and our tongue with singing. Then said they among the nations, 'The LORD has done great things for them.'" That's true today, too. The Lord has done great things, so let's laugh and enjoy!

📖 *Taking Action*

Take lots of fun breaks with your husband, children, and friends. Plan and prepare activities, but always leave a margin for God to map in His changes. Make a commitment to spend at least a half hour a day being unhurried. It will give you time to play.

List the things you can do to add more joy and laughter to your home life. Visit the library for joke books or storybooks. Watch a good cartoon with your child and try to see it through his or her eyes. Start making more time to play, and see the differences it makes. Post a sign on the frig: PLAY!

Prayer

Lord, how you loved children. I desire to be childlike in my trust of You. Help me enjoy the delights of life with my children. Help me heighten my sense of humor, enjoy simple pleasures, and relish the music and rhythm of life!

🐦 THIRTEEN 🐦
Choosing Ministry

A counseling client wanted more structure and purpose in her efforts for the Lord. I told her, "You already are a minister." She answered, "No way!" I explained ministry is the way you bring glory to God through the ordinary course of your life. If you're a daughter, a wife, a mother, an employer, or an employee, you already have a major ministry to glorify God in your very important roles.

Yet it's good to occasionally engage in self-examination. Let me explain. I'm a terrible singer; I once considered taking voice lessons to improve my singing — mostly so I would be comfortable in church situations that involved group singing. My motive was pride, not pleasing God or serving others. I don't know why God didn't gift me with a singing voice, but I do know He gave me other interests and strengths in the areas of counseling and writing to use on behalf of others.

In examining yourself, look at your motives for activities. Also look at your strengths and areas of interest. Is your purpose in seeking ministry opportunities to expand the church, please others, or receive personal praise? Or simply to help out because someone asked you? The best motive is to glorify God. It's the only motive worthwhile.

Caring for the unborn, the sick, those in prison, the poor, the parentless children — thousands of formal and informal ministries exist to meet these needs, and more help is always needed.

Some women have a powerful ministry providing the one home in the neighborhood where children can come after school to enjoy the presence of a caring mom. Many spontaneous neighborhood Bible studies have started like this — both among the children and the parents who have seen the love and care extended to their children.

The very fact that more help in the "harvest" is always needed, however, calls for a word of caution. A young woman named Jenna came in to see me, a dedicated Christian who also suffered from bulimia. She tended to say yes to every ministry-related task in her church that someone asked her to do. In reality Jenna couldn't handle all the "I'll do its" that she allowed into her life and as a result would become depressed. Eventually she'd grow frustrated and bow out of everything.

But soon she'd start over and become overwhelmed with commitments again. Jenna finally saw the relationship between eating too much food, then purging and overcommitting to responsibilities then purging activities at church. As so often happens, your body tells the real story. Your emotions can place impossible demands on you physically. Sooner or later your body will rebel. (This example doesn't mean every person who has bulimia overextends her commitments at church or elsewhere; this was simply Jenna's problem.)

Jenna's life was a smorgasbord. People in her life constantly wanted "talents and helps" from her. Jenna needed to take the time to examine her strengths and gifts and choose her ministry based on the strengths God had given her and His guidance. Jenna addressed this problem, and she was healed.

At the other extreme, one of my dearest friends struggled for years because she was greatly gifted by God to minister in the church body, but her gifts were not appreciated in her local church. Her self-image was deeply wounded. Eventually she tried to stifle some of her precious gifts and use other gifts in the business world. She ended up filled with frustration, anxiety, and using antidepressants. Some churches do not understand the place of women. They fail to study and apply Scripture's teachings about women. Christ has given women roles as His representatives within the church as well as without.

If you haven't been encouraged to get involved in your local church, talk humbly with the church leadership to see where you might be of help. If there is no place for you to serve there using the strengths God has given you, perhaps you can find a church that honors your involvement as Christ does.

Sometimes your ministries are recognized in your local church and community and have a wide outreach. Perhaps your ministry is known only to you and your coworkers That decision is up to God.

These principles may help you identify ministries God has designed specifically for you:

1. Write a list of the activities that give you the greatest satisfaction. Realize these leanings are from God. Next select your favorite three, listing first what you most enjoy.

2. Write a list of your positive qualities. Check the list with your friends. This is not bragging but is an opportunity to give glory to God by finding further areas for service.

3. Consider whether you most enjoy working alone, with one partner, or on a team.

4. Look to see what God is already doing and where you might fit in.

5. Ask the Holy Spirit to direct you to needs not yet being met that match your gifts.

6. Consider your time commitments. Will your ministry interfere with your time with Christ or your family?

7. Once you have identified your ministry, perform it. Don't procrastinate, yet don't overdo.

8. Continually be open to change. The strengths you use today may not be appropriate years from now. Every six months to a year, reevaluate your strengths and interests.

9. Many books and surveys are available for identifying your spiritual gifts. One of the greatest joys in the Christian life is identifying, applying, and developing the ministry gifts God has given.

10. Look for creative ways to use your strengths and interests in ministry in and out of church.

"Let your light shine before men." Consider more than the typical ministries of music and teaching in the church. For example, Janie is gifted in organization. She helps the young adults in her fellowship group by going to their apartments or homes to help them organize their papers, their kitchens, and their life. One young man raved his spiritual life had improved since Janie taught him to be more organized. He's now free of the drain of trying to manage a chaotic household and free to use his own gifts to better advantage. What helpful ministry he received!

Not every woman needs to take turns serving in the nursery or teaching Sunday school. I know it's hard to resist the pleas of the Sunday school superintendent, but by filling a job that you're not gifted or interested in, the task isn't joyful, and you may even be depriving others of the opportunity to minister through their gifts.

✒ Exploring Scripture

Colossians 3:23-24 says, "Whatever you do, work at it with all your heart, as working for the Lord, not for men, since you know that you will receive an inheritance from the Lord as a reward. It is the Lord Christ you are serving." (NIV).

- How should you minister and where do your rewards come from?

Galatians 1:10 says, "Am I now trying to win the approval of men, or of God? Or am I trying to please men? If I were still trying to please men, I would not be a servant of Christ" (NIV).

- God is pleased when you serve His people.

📖 Taking Action

- What creative gift(s) do you have that you've never used for the Lord?

- How might you use these gifts in your life now?

Brainstorm with other women friends about using your gifts and interests. You might be surprised at what they say!

Prayer

Dear Lord, I long to serve You with joy and with my whole heart. I want to hear Your voice some day telling me, "Well done." Help me to shut out the clamor of the demands of others and listen to You. May I minister well to my own family. Thank You for assuring me when I minister as You have designed, I please You.

🔊 F O U R T E E N 🔊
Controlling Your Image

*K*ristin is a beautiful woman who could be a model. Her husband feels lucky to have married her. She's a college graduate who worked as a flight attendant before she married. But she hid a secret that tormented her for years until she finally got brave enough to discuss it with me in counseling. She has a very poor self-image and believes everyone else is smarter, prettier, and more capable than she is.

Kristin is one of a shocking number of beautiful, talented women who suffer from feelings of inferiority. Perhaps some slight as a child at a sensitive moment of development fueled feelings of rejection, and she's never been satisfied with herself since.

Rejection has many sources. A woman can feel rejected because of a strong positive quality someone else envies. She can be rejected for her convictions. Perhaps she has been arrogant or unkind, and needs to learn better ways to relate to others. Perhaps she has bad habits of grooming or table manners through faulty training.

Being rejected can take the form of a subtle snub or extreme rudeness. But if you're to enjoy a healthy self-image, you must learn to deal with rejection because it's usually inevitable.

Look at the apostle Paul. His rejection was such that people wanted to kill him! Acts 14:19-22 describes how some Jews turned the minds of the people against Paul, stoned him, and "dragged him out of the city thinking he was dead." How did Paul deal with it? Paul got up and walked back into the city! Did it bother Paul's self-image greatly?

No. And the next day he was out preaching again, reminding the people that it is "through many tribulations that we must enter into the kingdom of God."

I explained to Kristin she may be poised, do everything "just right," have a "perfect" body, gorgeous clothes, and wear costly perfumes and still feel inferior. What she really needs is awareness of the beauty of holiness and the sweet fragrance of Christ.

God says over and over in His Word that you are precious. If you've never heard these words spoken with meaning by a parent or a spouse, you can hear God tell you whenever you set aside time to listen to Him. So act according to your worth to God — no matter how you may feel. He created you as you are and you are His. The choice is yours. God wants you to treasure yourself no matter what your background or current physical or financial status.

📖 *Exploring Scripture*

Luke 12:15 says, "...a man's [or woman's] life does not consist in the abundance of his possessions" (NIV).

- What part do possessions play in projecting your image?

📖 *Taking Action*

- Tell a close friend how you really feel about yourself. Ask the same friend what kind of image you project to others. Write her remarks here. Is that what you want to portray?

- List the good qualities others have said you have. Can you think of more?

Prayer

Lord, thank You for making me just the way You did. Help me concentrate each day on Your opinion of me and not the negative thoughts that readily enter my mind. Thank You for Your unconditional love and for valuing me enough to die for me. May I keep Your opinion of me uppermost in my mind.

FIFTEEN

Giving Testimony

Testimony means "firsthand authentication of a fact" according to Webster's dictionary. It's easy to give testimony about the facts of daily life.

In a spiritual sense, however, what is your testimony? What is the story of how God has reached you? Think about how you came to know Jesus. What were your doubts and fears? How has He helped change you? What is your testimony? Your personal story is the way you testify what God has done in your life is real.

I humbly share with you part of my own "testimony," the story of how God has acted in my life.

When I was twenty-eight I believed in a God who made me and made the world. Period. After the act of creation I believed He was out of the picture. On my own I had achieved all my childhood dreams of marriage and motherhood. I expected to live like a fairy-tale princess — "happily ever after." Instead, I often felt a vague emptiness. A sense of the meaninglessness of life confused me. Shouldn't life would be about something more? I sank into occasional depression.

I decided to search to find what, if anything, was of lasting value. I slowly realized that the emptiness of my life came from restlessness in my heart and that I longed for God.

I'd been a churchgoer brought up by a dad who took us to church regularly. My mom went to church only on holidays. God was never mentioned outside of church or my parochial school. After my children were born, going to church seemed like too much trouble, so I started finding excuses to stay home.

About this same time I was talked into going on a retreat — a neighborhood women's getaway weekend. Some of the women had dramatic experiences with God there. I didn't. But after the retreat for the first time I began studying about the Christian religion. Prior to that I'd studied Eastern religions and practiced yoga, not seriously but simply from curiosity. After the retreat I read Scripture and stories about people relating to God as if He were right here instead of a distant deity.

During this time, I became pregnant with my fourth child and had a medical crisis. I had to decide if I were willing to trust God with my life or not. I chose to believe that He loved me personally and had a plan for my life that was for my good and not for my harm.

I wanted to know more about His amazing power, so I studied and prayed. I ultimately decided to ask Jesus to be my Lord and repented of my sins of the past. I said, "God, if there's more of You than I know and understand, show me; I open my life to You." My life, which had become dulled after the achievement of many of my life goals, took on a vibrant spiritual purpose and became more exciting and joyful than I'd ever known.

Prior to that I'd always believed in a generic God — not in a God who cared about my every moment. Soon after I came to believe in God's personal care, my husband, Wayne, became a believer as well.

Somehow I pray that God has touched you also or that He soon will. What a joy to tell others and demonstrate God's love through your actions and words to every person you meet. Some people will be amazed at the love they see and want to know why you care for them. You and I need to be ready to describe how God desires to relate to each person individually.

Scripture is filled with the testimony stories of Christ's followers. You can study these accounts for help in preparing your own testimony. Pray about your encounters with others for Jesus whether it's with the clerk in the grocery story, the neighbor child who visits your home, or in a brief speech to anyone willing to listen. You may not automatically lead others to Christ, but your words may be an important step along someone's path.

The more you practice the more you can avoid being impersonal, mechanical, rigid, or insensitive, and focus on being tender, kind, and persevering. (See 32, "Leading Others to Christ.")

🖋 *Exploring Scripture*

Second Peter 3:9 says, "The Lord is... not willing that any should perish but that all should come to repentance."

- Why should you give your testimony?

Second Timothy 4:2 reads, "Preach the word! Be ready in season and out of season. Convince, rebuke, exhort, with all longsuffering and teaching."

- How can you apply Paul's command in this verse?

📖 *Taking Action*

Based on your personal experiences with Christ, perhaps you'll want to write your testimony to share with your family or others. Focus first briefly on your past, second on how you came to know Jesus, and the lastly describe what Christ has meant in your life.

Your testimony can include Scripture like:

- Romans 3:23: "For all have sinned and fall short of the glory of God."

- First John 1: 9: "If we confess our sins, He [Jesus] is faithful and just to forgive us our sins and to cleanse us from all unrighteousness."

- John 1:12: "But as many as received Him, to them He gave the right to become children of God, to those who believe in His name."

Prayer

Lord, thank You for my salvation through Jesus and for the joy You've given me. As I prepare my testimony, may I only include what is most pleasing to You and helpful to others.

‰⁓ SIXTEEN ‰⁓
Keeping Body and Soul Fit

*A*s I counsel female clients, two important areas I consider are physical health and spiritual health. Women often neglect their bodies and their souls resulting in depression, irritability with spouses, and feelings of inadequacy. Both bodies and souls atrophy from lack of exercise.

Overall we're a body-conscious generation. Women who used to make fun of high school gym classes now flock to health clubs and aerobics classes. Exercise helps women gain energy, feel better, and look better! Those who don't exercise often have tinges of guilt even as they tease friends who do!

In order to keep weariness from seeping into your bodies and souls, we need to set both physical-fitness goals for your bodies and spiritual-fitness goals for your souls and work consistently toward achieving them.

Body and soul goals are appropriate if they challenge you and are attainable and measurable. Physically your goals might be walking a mile or training to run a marathon. Spiritual goals might be daily prayer, reading three chapters of Scripture daily, getting through the Bible in a year, or memorizing one verse each week.

Along with setting physical and spiritual goals good nutrition is important. Nutritional goals correlate with physical and spiritual fitness goals. You need to select from all four food groups each day, use stimulants like caffeine only in moderation or avoid them altogether, and maintain proper levels of vitamins and minerals in your diet.

I counseled a young man in his late twenties who was suicidal. He couldn't understand how breakfast of sugared cereal, no lunch, and dinner at McDonald's five times a week was inadequate nutrition and would affect his appreciation of life. By improving his diet along with healing his emotional hurts through our counseling sessions, he was able to change his "victim" thought patterns and restore his enthusiasm for life.

I am continually amazed at how many of my clients do not eat healthy, well-balanced meals.

The hardest part is convincing clients that diet affects moods; it seems too easy. I explain to clients that they may not need extended counseling if they correct their nutrition. I suggest trying dietary changes during counseling. Afterward, the benefits become obvious to them.

You can check your spiritual diet the same way you check your physical diet. We're bombarded with suggestions to limit sugar and fat, increase raw fiber and fresh fruits, and eat food as close to the source as possible. Your study of God's Word should also be as direct as possible! Just as food loses nutrients during the refining processes, the personal meaning of God's Word can be lost when it's processed through others.

You eat meals three times a day. Are you willing to eat three spiritual meals a day too?

Here's a suggested spiritual menu:

- Breakfast: Using written prayer you can praise God for His holiness, faithfulness, and love and list the particular needs of the day.

- Lunch: Read an article or excerpt from a book or listen to a teaching tape - a great spiritual lunch. Tucking a small book into your purse and pulling it out at break time or lunch is a great witness. Keep a short devotional on your phone.

- Dinner: Another time for soul food is mealtime prayer with the family. Take turns discussing the highlights of each person's day with gratitude. Mention prayer requests where God's help might be necessary.

- Bedtime: Don't forget a bedtime snack! You'll sleep so much better! Just as sleep experts often recommend cereal or a piece of toast before bed, spiritual food helps you sleep better, too. You can ask God for one new truth or comfort from His Word before you end the day.

This will give you a steady diet of God the Father, Son, and Spirit all day long.

After spiritual and physical diet comes fitness activities. Notice I don't say exercise. Who wants to exercise? It doesn't sound like fun, more like work. But walk, play tennis, stretch, or play, it seems inviting. Find something you like to do and get out and do it!

You can ask other people to join you to make your exercise a social time or maybe a chance to minister to others. Young children might enjoy biking with you; a neighbor might enjoy walking with you.

Maybe it seems selfish to waste time on yourself. Wrong! Your body is the temple of the Holy Spirit. Consider the care the temple of Jerusalem required for upkeep. Are you less valuable? See 7, "Decorating Our Temples.") The

Lord is honored if you're a healthy weight, take care of your skin, and have a decent haircut regularly.

How do you get spiritual rest? Nature reflects the beauty and peace of God. Spend time outdoors. (See 12, "Playing Like a Child" and 29, "Refreshing Yourself.") Pray before choosing any new activity. Make changes in your lifestyles if you're sure God's in it. Avoid changes from pressure by others. You need to recognize the physical and spiritual benefits for yourself. Then you'll desire to make the changes.

📖 Exploring Scripture

Third John 2 reads, "Beloved, I pray that you may prosper in all things and be in health, just as your soul prospers."

How does this verse illustrate the connection between the body and the soul?

📖 Taking Action

- What are your physical fitness goals?

- List three steps you will take to reach your goals.

- What are your spiritual fitness goals?

- List three steps you will take to reach your goals:

Prayer

Lord, my body, mind, and spirit belong to You. Help me to care for them wisely —feeding, exercising, and resting them as a precious temple.

SEVENTEEN

Chasing Shadows

The shadow of worry can settle over a life. Chasing shadows is what is happening when you worry. Despite the prevalence of worry, I seldom have someone come into my office seeking counseling to get free of worry. Instead, clients want to remove every situation from their lives they worry over which is impossible.

Where does a tendency to worry come from? Ultimately it's sin — the same sin Eve knew, a desire to be in control, to know everything, and be like God. It filters through heredity and your environment.

Nancy revealed in counseling her mom had a tendency to often say, "I'm worried. I'm worried that my car won't start... that you'll be too cold in that coat... that..." Nancy picked up her "worry language" subconsciously from her mom.

Even more than the words themselves, Nancy picked up worry as a habitual way of responding. While some personality types — the more sensitive, deep thinkers who see the "what-ifs" around every corner — have a stronger temptation toward worry, outgoing, carefree personality types like Nancy have learned to worry by seeing parents use worry as a default way of responding to situations. When Nancy worried, she undermined her ability to realistically evaluate problems.

I observed a curious thing about worry in the women I've counseled. Many of these women could face the bigger issues of life such as a husband's illness or the loss of a home with greater inner peace and calm than minor problems. I believe this variation exists because God gives

60

grace to deal with the real trials of life, both large and small, so worry isn't necessary.

If you worry continually you're not experiencing God's grace in troublesome matters of life. Nancy got tied up with worry over trivial details. She was driving her husband crazy, and he insisted she get help. She came to see me supposedly about her marriage. In one session it was obvious worry had crept over every aspect of Nancy's life dimming her joy, confidence, and peace.

We studied the biblical principles regarding worry, Nancy was surprised to learn that worry is a sin and a temptation to worry must be resisted. I explained that worry is every bit as bad as overeating or self-centeredness and that worry damaged her relationship with God. You can't trust God totally and worry at the same time!

I encouraged Nancy to let tomorrow worry about itself. Of course tomorrow can't worry because it's not a person, which is probably why Jesus used the example. No worrying. Mother Teresa faced death from disease every day of her life for decades, yet she joyfully prayed and went about her business without a trace of worry.

Worry creates fear, and it's difficult to think and plan clearly when we have fear. That sneaky old Devil wants us to become locked in fear so we'll flop in our physical and spiritual and emotional life. As God's children, we need to tell him to get lost.

God tells us not to live in fear. Some gals hear accounts of husbands running off with other women and think, "That could be me. Can I really rely on his love?" Yes and no. You can always rely on God's love. You can't get a guarantee from a husband. All you can do is pray for your husbands' protection. If he's not a Christian, pray daily for his conversion and ask God to safeguard him in the meantime.

You can concentrate on being the kind of loving, sweet, affectionate wife no man in his right man would want to leave and forget your fears!

Worry is a dirty word! It's a temptation God knew we'd have. God made it perfectly clear how we are to deal with it — DON'T WORRY!! Refusing to worry is often an act of the will.

Look at Jesus, your supreme example. Jesus was fully human. Did He worry? No! He faced the future realistically, but not with worry. Jesus shed tears for us because we would reject His work of the Cross. There's no denying He said, "Let this cup pass." The night of His betrayal was an incredibly painful part of His sacrifice. Jesus was rejected by those He loved but He didn't spend His life prior to the Last Supper and the Crucifixion saying, "I'm so worried."

Jesus said in effect, "Hey guys, My betrayal and death are going to happen, so don't worry or be surprised." Jesus knew why He came. You know why you're here, too, to glorify God by your trust, to witness for Him, and to die. So why dread anything in life? After this life comes the "happiness forever" part.

✒ Exploring Scripture

Matthew 6:25-28 is the famous worry passage. "Therefore I tell you, do not worry about your life, what you will eat or drink; or about your body, what you will wear. Is not life more important than food, and the body more important than clothes? Look at the birds of the air; they do not sow or reap or store away in barns, and yet your heavenly Father feeds them. Aren't you much more valuable than they? Who of you by worrying can add a single hour to his life?" (NIV).

Take time to study this passage in different Bible translations to get the full impact of its meaning.

Notice Jesus taught the "Our Father" (Matthew 6:9-13) right alongside this passage. He said not to worry— pray and ask the Father to give you your daily bread, to protect you from evil.

As you remind yourself of God's holiness and power (hallowed be Your name), ask that only His will be done and remind yourself that His kingdom is coming. As you forgive and ask forgiveness, there's no worry that you're not in a right relationship with God the Father, Son, and Spirit. What a perfect antidote to worry! Trust in the Father!

📖 *Taking Action*

- What kind of things do you typically worry over? List them here.

- Will you commit yourself to be accountable to share with a friend your efforts to stop worrying? Write her name here.

- What are you to do when the urge to worry comes? "Don't worry over anything whatever; tell God every detail of your needs in earnest and thankful prayer, and the peace of God which transcends human understanding, will keep constant guard over your hearts and minds as they rest in Christ Jesus" (PHILLIPS). Philippians 4:6

- Write out the entire section Philippians 4:4-6 using your name in place of the pronouns. We take a powerful preventive measure when we allow God to help us not worry today. This is the kind of help the Holy Spirit gives us. Jesus told the apostles not to worry even about what they were to say if they were arrested. He said the Holy Spirit would tell them what to say.

Whatever the situation, rely on the Holy Spirit instead of worrying.

Prayer

Lord, my long list of worries does not come from You, for You give enough grace for each day. Thank You that You've told me over and over again that You love me and You are caring for me. Thank You that every day and every aspect of my life is in Your hands.

64

EIGHTEEN

Preventing Family Problems

*I*s there any greater pain than having a problem in your family? Psychologists describe the family as a system similar to the body made up of organs (family members). The system works best when all the organs are healthy and working together according to the same guidelines.

What are some of the guidelines that keep family systems running well? These counseling strategies will help you have smoother relationships with members of your families. As you read through each item, ask God to show you if it applies to you.

- If you don't expect any member of the family to think or act as you would, you won't be disappointed.

You can point out the advantages of a desirable action. If the other person is an adult, you need to state your expectation clearly once and avoid nagging. By all means pray, then let go of your desires and trust the outcome to God. If your children are still under your roof, you have more control, but they still have a free will. Modeling the behavior and values you'd like your children to display is the best method of teaching.

- Communicate clearly your feelings and needs to your husband and children and encourage them to do likewise. A client of mine in her late sixties never told her children when she needed their help with a chore or when she missed them. She expected her children to anticipate her needs and frequently said "They should know" and "If I have to tell them to help me, I'd as soon they not help me or come visit."

"Why?" I asked her. "With the busy lifestyle of your grown children, what's wrong with being direct with family close to you?"

- Be wary of providing "over care" for family members.

That means avoid repeatedly doing things for others they can do themselves. Over care can damage your relationships with the people you're helping, who may then begin to feel unnecessarily dependent and guilty. As long as you allow yourself to be used, you're tempting someone to use you. This is true of your children as well as your husband or extended family.

- Listen carefully to feelings family members express. Use common sense to evaluate their needs and decide how to respond — children who balk at going to bed don't benefit from staying up late, but as long as they can get away with it, they will.

- Make sure your self-image includes outlets besides taking care of others. Jesus says that you are significant to God simply because He loves you, not because of your works. Build an image of yourself that depends on what Jesus said and did for you and not on what you say and do.

- Avoid triangular conversation. If you tell your feelings to a son or daughter and want the child to communicate them back to your husband, an unfair burden is placed on the child who gets stuck in the middle. A child who doesn't want to relay a message risks feeling guilty and fears your anger. If they do express your concerns, they're worried their other parent will be angry or hurt.

- Take time to get emotional and physical rest. Be sure to stay alert to your personal needs or you won't be able to relate healthily to anybody else. Otherwise you can easily become resentful and exhausted as you meet others' needs and try to make those you love happy.

- Every family develops its own set of unspoken rules. Some of your family's rules may have come from your childhood without you even consciously thinking about it. These rules affect how you show joy, your anger, how you deal with stress or conflict, how you act toward others. Family rules are typically not spoken in words, but everybody hears them very clearly just the same. You need to examine them occasionally to see which are healthy and which, if any, you need to change.

Here are some examples of unhealthy family rules:

- Be a high achiever and make sure what you're doing is always productive.

- Work harder and work longer hours than necessary to get ahead.

- Deny your own feelings when someone else in the family is upset. (How can you think about yourself at a time like this?)

- Children, even when grown, are second-class citizens. Have you ever witnessed a successful businessman who acts the part of mommy's little boy when he goes to his home of origin? He's never allowed to be an adult around his parents.

- Talk only about what's pleasant. When someone makes a mistake, don't discuss it. Talk about abstract subjects like sports, world events, and jobs rather than personal issues.

- Focus your conversation on troubles and problems. When one member has a problem or disappointment, discuss it over and over and beat the topic to death.

- Be two different people. Swing between demanding to be pleased right now, and saying I don't care what you do.

The family should be a safe place where family members can admit weaknesses and not be laughed at or criticized — where family members always pull together not against each other. Alter any family rules that you no longer feel are right.

The Bible is the guidebook for rules your family systems should have. Your family can benefit from examining your family system in the light of Scripture regularly.

Some families would rather live in constant tension than risk change. Denial of problems keeps everyone walking on eggshells, often resulting in physical symptoms such as headaches, insomnia, and stomach pain that go along with family problems. Risk "being emotionally intimate" with your family. It's never healthy to isolate yourself.

🕮 Exploring Scripture

Read Ephesians 3:14-15: "For this reason I bow my knees to the Father of our Lord Jesus Christ, from whom the whole family in heaven and earth is named."

Where does the concept of family come from? The idea of family comes from God and belongs first to Him. We're part of His divine family. God ordained that a man and woman come together in marriage and become an indissoluble union.

🕮 Taking Action

Write down any unhealthy family rules that you need to change.
Are you presently dealing with a family problem?
Try handling it God's way:

1. Discuss it in love.
2. Do not be judgmental or critical.
3. Listen to and repeat aloud how the other person is feeling to make sure you understand correctly.
4. Brainstorm ways to solve the problem. Look for a solution agreeable to both sides.
5. Be willing to compromise out of love except on issues contrary to God's Word.

Prayer

Dear Lord, sometimes the voices of the past govern how I treat those I love today. Clear my mind and heart of destructive voices of my past, and help me to follow Your ways in keeping the relationships and communications healthy in my family.

NINETEEN

Giving Generously

A friend of mine occasionally pays highway tolls for herself and the car behind her when she goes through the tollbooth. She calls this a RAOK, a Random Act Of Kindness. Do you suppose her children sitting in the back seat are getting the idea? Generosity is a quality you teach best by modeling. How wonderful it would be if we all sprinkled our days with random acts of kindness! Even millionaires who give generously to others are blessed when they're treated generously by someone else.

As a Christian woman you know God should get a tithe, a tenth of the money that comes in the house. Still, as soon as things get financially tough, it can be tempting to skip this. Yet giving is essential in your Christian life - you get blessed as well! This is as true as gravity — if you give, you receive. What goes up comes down. I can't explain how it works, it just does. GIVE!! If your husband refuses to give, you can pray for God to change his mind and, in the meantime, look for other ways to practice generosity.

In America we're about to lose the last of the generation who lived through the depression and World War II. When there were few true jobs, people with money found odd jobs around their houses that those in need could do. Those jobs included paying neighbor women to bake bread for them rather than buying it from local markets or hiring men for garden work and cleanup. During the depression, government welfare provided food but not money. People looked out for one another with generosity and kindness. It was a unique time in our history.

To have extra finances to give to others, develop the quality of thriftiness. A thrifty person is not a hoarder or cheap but rather is a person who has a healthy perspective toward material possessions. Less can be better and inexpensive is fine as long as the quality is adequate. Recently I attended a lecture by a fashion consultant wearing a stylish outfit. She confided to the audience that she'd purchased everything, including her shoes, at a secondhand store.

You don't need lots of clothes, and you don't necessarily need expensive ones, to be neatly dressed and have a sense of confidence befitting a representative of Christ! When you shop, do you buy only sale items? God can afford to pay full price sometimes. There's a fine line between being a careful spender and being obsessive about bargains.

If an unexpected expense comes up, you might try saying, "Well Lord, instead of being discouraged, I'm going to find a way to give an extra gift to You."

Give generously of time and effort. Teach your children when they go to a public park or restroom to always leave the place a little better than they found it. Brainstorm ways to be generous to others! Work hard, save carefully, spend wisely, and give generously.

📖 Exploring Scripture

Proverbs 11:25 "The generous soul will be made rich, and he who waters will also be watered himself."

- In what ways can you become rich that don't involve money? 2 Corinthians 8:9 "For you know the grace of our Lord Jesus Christ, that though he was rich, yet for your sakes he became poor, so that you through his poverty might become rich" (NIV).'

- How's this for an example of God's grace?

- How does God's grace motivate you to be generous?

📖 Taking Action

- What can you do to practice more generosity in your home?

Prayer

Lord, there is a difference between thriftiness and being cheap, between generosity and being a spendthrift. Help me to know the difference and be both generous and wise.

TWENTY

Forgiving Others

The two greatest commandments are "Love the Lord, your God, with all your heart, soul, and mind, and love your neighbor as yourself." My client Leah needed to apply these commandments, but didn't take Scripture seriously, or she'd never have come to see me. You've probably dealt with anger over minor irritations. Leah had too, but when she came to see me, she was struggling with a feeling brand new to her as a Christian. Someone in her family had hurt her deeply, and that person refused to admit the wrong.

Leah became livid with rage whenever she thought of it, which was often, and the rage didn't go away over several months. Leah's exact words in describing her situation were, "Now I understand how someone can become angry enough with another person to desire to kill."

"Leah," I explained, "Jesus stressed the importance of forgiving because He knew Satan would use dissension to destroy people." Without blinking she answered, "I know, but I can't."

Can't? Leah was a mature Christian with forty years of walking with God, but she'd been deeply hurt. I asked her if she'd at least pray for the person who had wronged her. Leah looked as if I'd asked her to stick a knife in herself. She said this was impossible. She didn't know how she'd ever be able to pray for that person's good. I suggested she pray simply that God would deal with the individual with justice and mercy. Leah considered that and then agreed she could try.

73

Forgiveness is a basic principle of the Christian life, but it's hard to practice when it hits the area of a painful relationship. Praying for your enemies is the weapon God gives you to fight the temptations of Satan to hate your enemies and be filled with bitterness. Praying softens your heart so you can forgive. Leah finally accomplished this.

Christian testimonies are destroyed because a person won't forgive or pray for an enemy - anyone who has wronged you, whether real or perceived. Your prayers involve God in restoring rightness in your heart. This is basic in the Christian life and you need to apply it in situations where it seems impossible. That's what surrendering to the lordship of Christ over every area of your life means.

Won't people think you're weak and wimpy and letting people walk all over you if you're quick to forgive? So what? Forgiving shows greater strength and composure than reacting harshly to someone's personal attacks. Jesus said how important forgiveness is, "But if you do not forgive men their trespasses, neither will your Father forgive your trespasses." (Matthew 6:15).

When Carla's husband told her he didn't want to be married to her anymore, he said, "You can have the profit from the house." She said, "I'll be investing my share in another house, but I want you to know that I still consider this half your money. And when I do sell, you'll benefit too."

That's the love that makes people stop and think, What is it about these Christians? See how they love. Do they truly have a heavenly Father who watches out for them? Is forgiveness tough? You bet! By the grace of God it can be done.

Exploring Scripture

In John 8:1-11 real guilt encounters God's grace.

- Who are the "guilty" parties in this incident?

- Anybody perfect? I'm not. "Little" sins, "big" sins —
  they're all the same to God. Through the process of
  forgiveness, He gives us freedom to fix things up when
  we fail or somebody fails us. Jesus could say to each of
  us what He told the people who brought the adulterous
  woman to him "He who is without sin among you, let
  him throw a stone at her first" (John 8:7).

Taking Action

- Who has wronged you in the past or maybe is still
  offending you right now?

- Write a brief sentence promising to forgive the
  person(s) and pray for their welfare.

- Prayer is Part I. Part II is "do good to those who hurt
  you." That's even tougher, but ever so powerful. What
  good can you do for the person(s) listed above who has
  offended you?

Prayer

Lord, it's hard to forgive when I feel so used and deceived.
May Your grace and power flowing through me. Bring
forgiveness into my heart. Thank You for Your mercy, and
fill me with a loving heart and a willingness to be kind.

TWENTY-ONE

Imitating Great Women

Mentoring is a popular concept today. The Bible, timeless in its message, speaks of the value of mentoring in Titus 2:4, "That they [the older women] may teach the younger women to be sober, to love their husbands, to love their children, to be discreet, chaste, keepers at home, good, obedient to their own husbands, that the word of God be not blasphemed" (KJV).

Mentoring is the process of learning from a wise and trusted teacher. It can occur by studying the behavior of a person alive now or a historical figure like a woman from the pages of Scripture.

The "number one" model of womanhood in the Bible is Mary, the mother of Jesus. God thought highly of this woman to choose her for His divine conception! What qualities can we learn from her life? Imagine the anguish and confusion of Mary as she stood at the cross and heard Jesus say, "It is finished" then dropped His head and died as she stood watching His agony.

Perhaps Mary thought, "Gabriel, you didn't mention this part. This wasn't the end I expected." Mary, above all others, knew the power her Son possessed. Perhaps she saw private miracles before the wedding at Cana, or she wouldn't have asked Jesus to perform a winemaking miracle.

Mary knew Jesus had power over the cross. Yet she watched Him choose to endure it and the Father allowed Mary's Son to die in her presence. But the angel Gabriel had said Jesus would occupy the throne of David? Mary also may have expected an earthly king. How could Mary make sense of that?

How did she respond? In steadfast obedience, Mary continued to do the things expected of her. She went to pray with the apostles after Jesus' death. Acts 1:14 says, "They all joined together constantly in prayer, along with the women and Mary the mother of Jesus, and with his brothers" (NIV). She continued to trust God. Wouldn't you have loved to witness her joy when she saw Jesus alive again!

A client of mine, the wife of a prominent local businessman, lost two sons four years apart, but she never lost her belief in a loving, powerful God. I can only imagine her joyful reunion with her sons in heaven some day! In the meantime this woman goes right on keeping on. Is this a powerful message to those around her? You bet.

You may know God has the power to change difficult situations you're going through right now, and you wait and wait for Him to act, but He doesn't. Can you keep on keeping on? What kind of model of womanhood do you want to provide for your children and your children's children?

📖 Exploring Scripture

In the lives of other great women described in Scripture, you'll see more qualities worth imitating.

Esther 4:1 When challenge came into Esther's life, she was ready.

Luke 8:2 Mary Magdalene's life teaches that nothing in our past can prevent us from loving and serving Christ.

Judges 4:4-5 Deborah was a wise, talented woman who demonstrated creativity and leadership as a judge.

Ruth 1:1-4:22 Ruth was persistent and steadfast.

📖 *Taking Action*

- If your life were written up as a Bible story, what would it say about you? Write a brief paragraph.

Prayer

Lord, I need to be mentored and I need to be a mentor for others. Give me eyes to see the best examples in those around me, and help me never forget others are watching me.

✎ T W E N T Y - T W O ✎
Sanctifying Your Home

O ne night I dreamed about young children asleep in beds with headboards molded into plastic half-wheels with wide spokes. Each child's name was at the center of their half-wheel. Scripture verses, uniquely applying to each child's life, were hand-printed on each spoke.

This dream signified to me a command God gave all parents in Deuteronomy 6. You've been ordered to diligently teach God's Word to your children, the neighborhood children, and your grandchildren. The Jews use a mezuzah (a tiny scroll containing these verses) attached on their doorposts, which they touch every time they enter their home to remind them of God's Word in verse 9: "You shall write [His commands] on the doorposts of your house and on your gates."

Why should you sanctify your home? To dedicate it as a place where others can experience God. When we moved from one home to another, we had a house dedication ceremony with our friends. My husband and I, our children, our pastor, and Christian friends walked through our home, stopping frequently to pray and dedicate it to God. If you haven't already asked God's blessing upon your home, I strongly urge you to do so.

As a reminder, at the garage door entrance and on the deck, in prominent places, we've posted the words contained in Joshua 24:15, "As for me and my house, we will serve the Lord." When our daughters married, we purchased housewarming gifts with this verse written on refrigerator magnets and wall hangings.

The music, the pictures, the books of your home can advertise Christ to your children and inspire your guests. I recently visited the National Gallery of Art in London, England, and was reminded again that the majority of great art has had a Christian theme for centuries. Not every picture in your home has to have a specifically Christian theme, but certainly several should.

My friend Kathy has decorated her living room and kitchen along the theme of the vine and the branches. (John 15:5-8) She has ivy wallpaper, and a local artist painted ivy on one of her walls. Her other decorations tie the theme together exquisitely. Whenever anyone comments, Kathy explains the story of the vine and the branches and her position of clinging to Christ.

In Deuteronomy 6:6 God commands talking about the Word at meals, discussing Bible principles at bedtime and throughout the day, and making your home a place where others can grow closer to God. We used to keep a box of Bible verses on the kitchen table and have each child pick a verse (read it for the little ones) and talk about how it applies to their day.

You can discover triggers that remind You of God's love and presence in your home and in your mind and heart and your children's - not just cultural trappings of Christianity but springboards for thought and prayer. Otherwise it's easy to forget about the centrality of Christ.

In daily conversation you can help your children appreciate God's signs around them. Point out the hand of God in things like sunsets, cloud formations, and storms. You can enjoy the beauty of people and point out their fascinating features.

📖 Exploring Scripture

John 14:23 "Jesus answered and said to him, 'If anyone loves Me, he will keep My word; and My Father will love him, and We will come to him and make Our home with him.'"

- What is the source of your home's holiness?

- Psalm 127 is the Scripture we used for our home dedication. What does it say about our work and about family?

📖 Taking Action

- Make a list of the steps you will take to dedicate your home to the Lord.

- What additional meaningful symbols or actions can you use in your home to remind you that your body, your home, your life is sanctified for God?

Prayer

Lord, be present in our home, filling it with Your love and wisdom. I want to decorate our home with those pictures and ornaments that daily increase my knowledge and awareness of You, and may I never forget that our home is dedicated to You.

ॐ TWENTY-THREE ॐ
Keeping the Joy

*A*rlene, a thirty-year-old mom, came to see me because she'd lost her zest for life. I've often seen this listlessness in moms who felt trapped by childcare and work. I've also seen it in older women with grown children who thought they'd be happy in their later quiet years and instead have become irritable and depressed, and I've seen this lack of joy and listlessness in single women who long for a husband and a family.

Whatever your age or circumstances, here are tips to keep joy in your life at any age.

- You can choose to keep your joy.

Irritations can steal emotional joy. Every day some things will happen that can get you in a dither. Sometimes you can take action to correct them, but often you must simply commit yourself to keep a joyful spirit despite your circumstances.

- You can maintain joy and seek beauty and harmony no matter what.

Keep your inner self cheerful and pleasant by finding something to enjoy in every moment — the beauty in the rays of the sun illuminating a room, a cloud formation, someone's smile, the colors of fresh vegetables in a salad, or even the smell of a fragrant cleaning product!

Our son David was diagnosed with cancer, and four months later, while out jogging, he was hit by a drunk driver. The accident shattered his leg and put him in a thigh-high cast. He and I spent 160 days in the hospital in one year. Every day we found something to smile, chuckle, and sometimes even laugh about. We chose to refuse to lose your joy. Thanks be to God, he was healed.

- You can sprinkle your life regularly with new experiences.

A new experience can be exciting whether it's a book you read, a first day as a volunteer, a change in your recreation, a day's outing, or a new blouse. Of course a long vacation qualifies, but the new experience doesn't have to be elaborate. It's always fun to have some event you're planning for the future. Often the waiting is therapeutic as is the experience. The side benefit of new experiences is that you have interesting stories to share with the people around you. You don't need to settle for a humdrum life.

- Experience joy in God's Creation, in His people and His dynamic plan for your life. Focus on the present and future. The past is never again. It's full of pain, mistakes, injustices, those you caused and those done to you. You can mentally beat yourself over the past or let it go.

If you have a physical limitation, try not to dwell on it; everyone has something.

Chances are the people close to you have heard enough. Keep on doing what you can. You can choose to refuse to lose your joy.

- When you need to make a decision, pray first and then follow your natural inclinations and don't stew over decisions.

Many young women I counseled got tied in knots because of indecision. I suggested doing what seemed to be the next right, logical step. Don't stew and huff and puff over every little thing. Of course, research your options as best you can. Some choices will be "wrong," but most are not really worth groaning over. Far better to get on making good new choices. Choose to refuse to lose your joy.

Decision-making can take far too much time. One gal said she used to spend ten minutes studying the menu in a restaurant and then usually order something she didn't like as much as the entree served to someone else at her table. Skim the menu and make a decision. I'd rather enjoy the company of the people I'm with or the book I brought to read if I'm alone.

- You can find a measure of satisfaction in the work you must do now. You can learn to do it well, whether it's working on the assembly line or designing fashions. Each day you are alive you can be aware of your senses as you work. You can enjoy the feel of the pen or the computer keys, the texture of the bags you fill, or the arm you stick an IV needle into.

Take time to smile at a baby and be pleased with the wiggles and stretches when you try to change a diaper. Be happy that your health allows you to be active. Finding pleasure in work is therapeutic. Just because you must do something doesn't mean you can't choose to enjoy it. Balance your work with an activity you love, like creating or collecting something for a hobby. Choose to refuse to lose your joy.

- Be satisfied with who you are, and what you're able to afford financially. Make a habit of satisfaction, not dreary resignation.

Even if you can afford a nice speedboat, it's fun to experience the pleasure of a rowboat or a canoe occasionally. Even if you can afford to eat at gourmet restaurants every night, you can try a picnic in the park now and then. Explore the library and museums for music, art and stimulating ideas. Take up an inexpensive hobby. Finding free and inexpensive sources of joy keeps you free from dependence on money for pleasure. Choose to expand your joy.

📖 Exploring Scripture

Jesus didn't sit in one place. He was often on the go, traveling to new places, meeting different people. He's your model. Get involved and stay active.

How did Jesus feel about joy? Great attitudes in the Bible are recorded in Matthew 5:1-12 and Luke 6:20-23. In effect, these verses say: When you don't have enough money, you're hungry or sad, or people are against you and reject you, when things aren't going well, "Rejoice in that day and leap for joy [When? Then, in that day, when it's happening!] for indeed your reward is great in heaven" (Luke 6:23). In so doing you choose joy.

📖 Taking Action

- Have you lost your joy in any of the areas described? Record what steps you will take now to make the necessary changes in your attitude and lifestyle to keep your joy.

- Think of ways you can teach your children to live joyfully, no matter what.

Prayer

Lord, living a joyful life is a decision I make. Help me daily to see opportunities for joy around me and savor the joy that comes from You.

TWENTY-FOUR

Releasing Creativity

Y ou're creative because you're made in the image and likeness of God, the Creator of all things. God created everything and everyone.

Unless you look for opportunities to be creative, you'll mainly be consumers of the creativity of others. Unfortunately, that's not emotionally satisfying enough for children or adults because you have an innate need to use your talents. Being creative is psychotherapeutic; not creating is a deprivation. How then can you release the creativity within?

Cooking, collecting, journaling, crafting, gourmet cooking, home decorating, paper folding, painting, writing letters or poetry are all proven creative outlets. You can try them all to see what you love doing the most.

Ever wonder why food has to be prepared? Couldn't God have given us food that didn't have to be peeled, trimmed, chopped, sliced, and sometimes cooked? Sure! But quite possibly He knew we'd need the creative satisfaction that preparation allows. Combine, spread, smush. Cooking can be very creative, and its also a fun way to teach creativity to your children. Although many of the past avenues for creativity such as cooking, sewing, and weaving are no longer essential, they're still worth doing for fun.

Creativity doesn't have to be costly. Deciding how to make do with what you have can be a creative activity — I used to like cutting off my boy's outgrown long pants to make shorts when summer came. When you gather for a family party instead of having the adults visit together while the children play, try to have at least some activities where adults and children interact.

The last weekend in October our family celebrates fall. This past year we went on a leaf hunt. My sister, Joy, and I gave her son and each of my five grandchildren a bag and went for a walk in the woods to find ten gorgeous leaves.

Then we returned to the house and gathered around the table. Each child had an adult to help, and we passed out finger paint paper and gobs of paint. After smearing around some background colors, each child stuck the leaves decoratively on the paper.

The results were not Michelangelo worthy, but the children will remember our activity because it was creative and we did it together. What a great chance to enjoy God's beauty and grow closer as a family.

Creative fun takes a tiny bit of thinking ahead. Preschool activity or school art books can provide ideas. If your children see you enjoying a creative activity, they'll be more likely to want to participate on their own. When our children were little, I was a full-time homemaker and I sewed most of their clothes. My daughters wanted to sit with me and make doll clothes and eventually their own clothes.

Collecting can be a creative enterprise. I've seen beautiful collections of salt and pepper shakers or glass bottles. Some people decorate with a theme of an animal or a fruit and collect roosters or cows or strawberries. Everyone can get involved in the fun of buying items to add to their collections, and they don't have to be expensive original art.

Some women find time to play an instrument; others write music. Having a creative hobby they love enhances rather than detracts from their child-rearing and homemaking roles.

You may want to keep a journal not only for the therapeutic value of recording feelings but also for the creative task of putting words on paper. How many Louisa May Alcotts are out there?

My husband Wayne wrote a poem when we visited the lakes area of England, and I read the poem to our grandsons. Six-year-old Jack now carries a notebook around with him and writes his own poems. Had we never introduced this to Jack, would he ever have gotten excited about writing poetry? I doubt it. We have fun hearing Jack read his poems to us over the phone. His mom helps him write them down, of course.

My mother taught me to be creative. In grade school I wanted to dress like everyone else, wear the same colors and even the same style clothes. Mom said over and over, "Be different, be yourself; you don't have to look, act, and think the same." And my father encouraged me to try different jobs and activities. He subtly communicated he was sure I could do anything. My parents passed an eagerness to be creative on to me. This is what I want to give my family.

✐ *Exploring Scripture*

Creativity is such an important activity that the Bible begins and ends with it! Genesis 1:1 tells us, "In the beginning God created the heavens and the earth." And then Revelation 21:5 says, "then He who sat on the throne said, 'Behold, I make all things new.' And He said to me, 'Write, for these words are true and faithful.'"

📖 *Taking Action*

Come up with a creative activity you can try alone and another one to try with your children. How about encouraging your children to write or tell stories? Help them compose a poem or put on a play for Grandma.

How about a craft project? Make Barbie or GI Joe doll furniture out of boxes. An egg carton section makes a nice footstool. For creativity in the kitchen, let your children make smiley faces or animal features on fruit or sliced bread. Use raisins or pineapple with mayo for gluing food on other food. Carrot shreds and coconut make fun hair. Make sailboats and rafts out of bread and cheese. Thank God for creating colorful, richly textured, and nourishing foods as you create your own delicacies. If something turns out especially nice, encourage your children to repeat the creation for a family gathering.

Be silly, be imaginative, and have fun. Your son(s) as well as your daughter(s) will enjoy sharing in creative activities.

Releasing creativity is one of those areas where you simply have to do it before you can evaluate whether you have a creative bent. What creative activity would you like to try?

Prayer

Lord, enable me to see the possibilities of things I can make in the world around me. Help me to think creatively and to share these ideas with my children. Keep me out of the rut of always doing things the same way.

TWENTY-FIVE

Pleasing God

G ood news! God wants you to know that you are pleasing to Him as you are and He delights in you! It's not what you do but what's been done by Jesus that makes us lovable.

Wow! That means, among other things, you can quit trying so hard to please God and bask in being loved. It's natural to want to please Him, but you can easily drift away from God if you feel you can never do enough to please Him.

A recent TV performer has the right attitude. She said, "I've never felt apologetic about my faith or my career; it's the Lord I want to please, not critics or 'religious' people."

Some women are too intent on keeping family members in their lives happy to think about pleasing God. Angie was an older woman going through change-of-life and given to bouts of depression. I was the fourth psychotherapist she consulted. Angie needed marriage counseling - her husband refused. Through counseling Angie quit focusing excessively on pleasing her husband despite his indifference to her. She put her personal priority on pleasing God. Finally, she found contentment.

Angie also had a critical mother who constantly nagged her. Angie needed to confront her mom, but was afraid. Angie felt trapped until she fully surrendered responsibility for making her mother happy to her mother and God.

God's love for you is unconditional and not performance-based.

🖋 Exploring Scripture

Psalm 16:3 says, "As for the saints who are on the earth, 'They are the excellent ones, in whom is all my delight.'"

- How does God's delight in us provide security?

James 4:7-8, 10 says, "Submit yourselves, then, to God. Resist the devil, and he will flee from you. Come near to God and he will come near to you. Wash your hands, you sinners, and purify your hearts, you double-minded... Humble yourselves before the Lord, and He will lift you up." (NIV).

- What are some attitudes and actions that specifically please God?

📖 Taking Action

If you've confessed your sins, asked God to guide your life, and try to live by His Word, you're pleasing to God! Whatever your past, Jesus forgives.

You're a straight-out saint according to 1 Corinthians 1:2: "To the church of God in Corinth, to those sanctified in Christ Jesus and called to be holy, together with all those everywhere who call on the name of our Lord Jesus Christ — their Lord and ours" (NIV). This may sound shocking. Sainthood doesn't necessarily involve doing miraculous things for God. It's living in, for and through Christ.

Think of Christians you recognize as saints now on earth even with their human frailties.

Reading this book is evidence of your desire to please God. Sit alone with your eyes closed and picture God as a Father teaching you to walk and encouraging you when you fall. Over and over God helps you back on your feet and heads you in the right direction. He knows you're not able to stand alone. He stays nearby to catch you. Pleasing God is easy. Just take your little steps. He delights in you.

Prayer

Dear Heavenly Father, please help me keep my eyes on You and my desire to please You foremost. Thank You for the specific encouragement You give me in Your Word. I love You more and more each day.

TWENTY-SIX
Protecting Faith

Your children will come in contact with other religious beliefs. Perhaps they'll hear that faith is a crutch for people who are fearful or insecure and God is unnecessary - they can run their own lives quite well.

Post-midnight discussions at slumber parties in high school or in college dorms are fertile ground for lost faith unless your children are well informed. Many young people lose their faith in God from arguments that sound good, but are false.

Clothe your children with the spiritual truths the right size for their ages just as you clothe them with physical garments that fit. Hosea 4:6 warns, "My people are destroyed for lack of knowledge." Your children need to learn how to effectively counter arguments like "Everybody's opinions and beliefs are as valid as anybody else's." "Religion is a cultural belief; culture changes." "Your faith is old-fashioned and outdated."

Some say faith is believing what you know isn't true! Or believing what you can't know! Both those statements are false. Faith is a reasonable belief system. Get the facts about other religious beliefs and cults first and be prepared to answer questions. Don't be deceived; protect yourself and your children. Keep a collection of books on hand to supply answers you don't have. You can protect your children as you educate yourself.

Teach your children belief in a personal God is relevant to their daily lives. Do your children think God keeps a scorecard of their good and bad deeds? I used to think that was true, and I wouldn't know until time for heaven if I could get in or not. Faith is not a set of rules followed to become good.

Other faiths may contain part of the truth. Confusion often comes from ignorance of what Jesus actually said and did. A friend told my husband recently he couldn't believe in Jesus because Jesus never claimed to be God. He was dead wrong, as Scripture reveals.

You can easily make a strong historical case for the credibility of God's Word, the Bible, but the best proof is changed lives. Addicts get set free; men get touched by the Holy Spirit and return to their families. We've met people so close to Christ that their faces glow when they speak of Him.

These are signs of Jesus' power among us still.

🖋 Exploring Scripture

Second Corinthians 10:5 "We demolish arguments and every pretension that sets itself up against the knowledge of God, and we take captive every thought to make it obedient to Christ." (NIV).

What does this verse tell you to do to guard your faith?

How does God help you protect and share your faith? In 1 John 5:13 we read, "These things I have written... that you may know..." and in Philippians 2:13 we read, "...it is God who works in you both to will and do for His good pleasure." God wants His children to know Him and has given the Bible as a source of truth. What a relief to have God working in you!

📖 Taking Action

Role-play with someone who takes the role of a nonbeliever. Practice until you can respond to their objections. Use Scripture to back up your statements. Have your children practice until they're comfortable explaining and defending their beliefs.

For further study read *Surprised by Faith* by Don Bierle, *Mere Christianity* by C. S. Lewis, and *Evidence That Demands a Verdict* by Josh McDowell. Discuss these books with your children. Your best defense against the attacks that will inevitably come is being well prepared.

Prayer
Lord, there will always be those who do not love You and seek to destroy faith in You. Keep me studying Your Word diligently. Give me knowledge and understanding of You and Your Word, both for myself and for teaching Your truths to my children.

TWENTY-SEVEN
Celebrating Often

*F*ifty-year-old Wanda existed in a web of routine broken only by interruptions to meet the needs of her children or friends. She'd worked hard as a child and never expected to do less as an adult. She grew accustomed to always having some chore just ahead that demanded her attention.

As a child, Wanda never went out much or was encouraged to get involved in outside activities. In fact her nervous, fearful mother acted as if something horrible would happen to Wanda when she went out. It was easier for Wanda to stay home than deal with her mother's tension.

After she married, Wanda lived near her parents' home. At first Wanda's husband tried to get her enthused in his sports interests. He eventually gave up. She thought money spent on recreation was frivolous. She seldom called friends. They were probably just as busy as she was and wouldn't want to be disturbed. And she rarely entertained because of the extra work and expense.

Wanda wasn't much fun to be around, and her husband and two children often left her home alone while they went out. She didn't mind; she could get more done without them around. When Wanda had spare time, she'd tackle some extra household project and then complain about her drudgery.

The biblical story of the Prodigal Son in Luke 15 is about a joyless elder brother — perhaps a lot like Wanda.

The story focuses on the younger son and the father's joy when the son repents of his wrong ways and returns home, but the father's elder son wasn't thrilled to see his disobedient younger brother treated like royalty. The elder son had plodded along day-by-day being the good guy, priding himself on his faithful diligence. Do you get the impression that the eldest's lifestyle must have been a drudge?

Why was it unusual for the elder son to hear music and dancing coming from his house? Whose fault was it the elder son hadn't had parties there for his friends? He never stopped to enjoy the benefits he had? The dad, who symbolizes God in the story, said to the elder son, "Everything I have is yours. All you had to do was ask."

✎ Exploring Scripture

Luke 15:28-31 in Phillips' translation reads, "Then he [the elder son] burst out: 'Look, how many years have I slaved for you and never disobeyed a single order of yours, and yet you never gave me so much as a young goat, so that I could give my friends a dinner! But when that son of yours arrives, who has spent all your money on prostitutes, for him you killed the calf we've fattened!'

- What can you learn about the lifestyle and expectations of the "good" older son?

- The dad says in verse 32: "We had to celebrate and show our joy." When was the last time you celebrated your joy?

- Does your life indicate that you know how to celebrate the blessings in your life?

📖 *Taking Action*

- If you're not having good times regularly, what keeps you from celebrating joyfully with your husband and your family?

- Check which attitudes apply to you (and which attitudes you're giving your children):

__1. You feel guilty when you're not productive.

__2. You feel like you don't deserve special times.

__3. You feel convinced you can't afford to have fun.

__4. You feel it's wrong to spend money for frivolity.

__5. You feel fun is a waste of time.

__6. You're drifting through your days, not planning ahead.

__7. You're lazy about following through on making arrangements.

__8. You expect others to make suggestions and plans for you.

__9. You're bitter that others seem to have more fun than you.

__10. There's nothing to celebrate.

- Ask God if anything is holding you back from celebrating and enjoying your life more. Is there an attitude you have or something within your circumstances you can change?

Prayer

Father, You have given me work to do on behalf of You and others, and You've also given me many reasons to celebrate. Give me a grateful heart to celebrate the joys You give. Free me from the routine of drudgery and make my spirit joyful and happy.

TWENTY-EIGHT

Being Real

What kind of image do you project? Are you a super religious, pseudo-perfect specimen of a woman no one can identify with?

We're all imperfect humans. We sin and need to repent frequently. We all need encouragement to grow as Christians. When Jesus was around other people, He didn't intimidate them. Many thought He was cool. They may have said, "Let's invite Jesus because He's fun to visit with and tells fascinating stories," or "Let's ask Jesus another question and see what He thinks." People were comfortable around Jesus. They knew He was for real.

Jesus didn't hide what was important to Him. He enjoyed his time with people but it didn't interfere with his private time with His Father for prayer. Yet he didn't cajole others to follow suit, "Okay guys everybody come out to the hills with me for prayer time." No. He simply did what was important to him without flaunting or fanfare. Jesus didn't nag or pester.

How about you? Do you wake up each morning thinking I can't wait to talk to the Father - another day to praise the Lord and serve Him!" Is this your attitude? Or do you call yourself a Christian and go about your life as if Jesus didn't matter at all? If your relationship with God is important, what are you doing about it?

You can't live for the Kingdom that begins on earth unless you're willing to mingle with people. It's scary to be real. You become one of the bunch on the front line with other real people struggling with confusion and sinfulness. You can be strong enough spiritually and emotionally to be real only if you keep your relationship with the Father super tight.

All God's people are sinners as well as saints. Jesus loves us extravagantly — enough to die for all. I've found after I've formed a friendly relationship with someone and presented God's truth in a loving way, if my acquaintance chooses to remain in a sinful lifestyle, I move on to other friendships, but try to keep the doors open. I excuse myself from frequent companionship. By staying in close contact with the Father, I've found Him faithful in letting me know when to back off and when to continue friendship.

I think of Jesus's words to the rich young ruler, "You asked what you need to do to get into the kingdom. I've answered you. The choice is yours."

Intimacy means "In To Me See." If you admit your faults to others, they can know who you really are — an imperfect person trying to improve – you become a safe person. Scripture recommends confessing our sins to one another. If you're willing to give up the pretense of perfection, people around you become comfortable showing their true selves.

✒ Exploring Scripture

The Phillips translation describes Jesus' intense feelings in Mark 14:33-34: "He took with Him Peter, James and John and began to be horror-stricken and desperately depressed. 'My heart is nearly breaking,' he told them."

Can you identify with this image of our Lord? It's real. Jesus wasn't afraid to share feelings — angry, sad, rejected, disappointed, and betrayed by His close friend. Jesus felt emotion and showed it. He survived these emotions by turning to His Father in heaven. I teach counseling clients to do exactly this. Feel your emotions deeply, and then move on. Don't get stuck in them.

Look up Luke 7:36-50. Jesus was invited to have dinner with Simon, a Pharisee, one of the religious leaders investigating who Jesus was. Jesus attended. It was a chance to reach Simon. While there, Jesus allowed a woman, a known sinner, to wash His feet, a woman Simon thought shouldn't be touching a holy man. Jesus straightened Simon out. He came to save sinners.

📖 *Taking Action*

- Do you spend time with sinners and present the truth of Jesus?

- When you're together, do they know you're like them except for the righteousness Christ gives?

- If you befriended an alcoholic, a prostitute, or a homosexual, how would this go over at your church?

Prayer

Heavenly Father, You know me as no person on earth knows me. You see me with all the gifts and talents You've given me, and You see me struggle with my shortcomings and doubt. May my life lead others to You as they see the honesty and freshness only You can give.

ᔆᐤ TWENTY-NINE ᔐᔒ
Refreshing Yourself

D ealing with physical weariness is difficult, but you
know how to handle this — get extra rest, reduce
stressful demands, adjust your schedule. Handling emotional
and spiritual weariness is more difficult.

Can people be fulfilled without Christ? Yes and no.
Perhaps temporarily, but not eternally. A client struggled
with discipline in prayer and Bible study. She was rebuffed
in sharing her faith with her brother and sister-in-law. They
said, "We're glad you found something meaningful to you,
but we're happy with our life the way it is." Her relatives
were carefree, traveled in their free time and even
occasionally helped others, not as an act of service in Christ
but simply as an altruistic thing to do. My client concluded
people can be fulfilled without God and began questioning
the time she spent doing "God stuff" in her life.

It's natural to want an answer for non-Christians'
apparent success and satisfaction. You want non-Christian
friends and relatives to have happiness, but it gets confusing
when they seem so content or successful while you struggle
at times. My client and I considered these issues.

1. Are non-Christians truly as happy as they profess?
Some wear a mask. In counseling I often glimpse confusion
and pain behind the smiling facade.

2. No one wishes misfortune upon another person, but
trials do come. Sometimes seeming happiness is built on
sand. The house may look great, but adversity can prove it
isn't. Jesus warned about building on shifting sand.

3. Non-Christians can be happy, but would they be far happier if they knew the God of the universe?

I don't have all the answers, but I know comparison is never healthy. The important thing is how can you refresh yourself spiritually? What helps me refresh myself is my Scripture arsenal. You need at least one, maybe two or three, awesome encouragement verses. Memorize the words to carry them with you wherever you go. You can whisper them into your heart when you're in difficult situations. The Word is like an injection of nitroglycerin— fast-acting, recharging, and refocusing. God's Word works! When you just want a minute alone and can't get one, you can go into the privacy of our own mind.

When you have time for a longer pick-me-up, read Psalms. As you meditate on the words the psalmist used to describe almighty God, you can pick something poetic, practical, striking, forceful — whatever appeals to you and gives you an image of God that you like to think about.

Fall asleep at night repeating a verse to yourself and thinking about its meaning. Using a special verse calms you when you're driving through stalled traffic or when waiting in line with groceries for dinner. A special verse for a morning prayer can help motivate you to get going.

You may already know that it's helpful when going though any time of trial to review what God's word says about His help, His presence, and His support. But do you run there first before calling a friend? Sound too simple, too naive? People I counsel through grief, financial distress, or rebellion of a child are intensely comforted by memorizing a significant Scripture verse fitting their situation. Speak the Word and meditate on it often.

📖 *Exploring Scripture*

Morning, noon, and night, refresh yourself in God's Word. Form your own collection of Scripture treasures. Women have a heart-chord for beauty. Surround yourself with beautiful thoughts and exquisite ideas whatever your budget! The "furniture" in the private room of your mind can be as fine as any Queen's!

Here are some of my favorites. Pick your favorite "soul sunshine."

- "May the favor of the LORD our God rest upon us; establish the work of our hands for us — yes, establish the work of our hands" (Psalm 90:17 NIV). Believe me, this is a great mindset for starting a day!

- "He who dwells in the shelter of the Most High will rest in the shadow of the Almighty. I will say of the LORD, 'He is my refuge and my fortress, my God, in whom I trust'" (Psalm 91:1-2 NIV). This is a great help for going through the day.

- "Praise the LORD, O my soul; all my inmost being, praise his holy name. Praise the LORD, O my soul, and forget not all his benefits" (Psalm 103:1-2 NIV). Start listing all His benefits and blessings one by one, and you'll be asleep before you can finish.

If you go by God's clock, you'll never become impatient.

"For a thousand years in your sight are like a day that has just gone by, or like a watch in the night."
(Psalm 90:4).

📖 *Taking Action*

Memorize one verse per day or one a week — medical research confirms the physical benefit of using your minds to keep them sharp and clear. This isn't surprising. Using every part of the body keeps it healthy. There are a lot of dull minds running around in healthy bodies. I see many women for counseling who skip time to think and time to pray from their lives because of crammed schedules, who become resentful and emotionally and spiritually exhausted.

- What circumstances make you spiritually weary?

- Select one verse you will commit to memorize and use as a lift to your spirits, and keep hidden in your heart for just such a time, and write it here:

Prayer

Lord, Your Word refreshes my spirit. Your truth, Your encouragement feeds me. The weariness and baggage of this life fall away, and I am renewed. I need to bask in the Word, like soul sunshine.

THIRTY

Surviving Your Husband's Life Crises

W hat's commonly called a male midlife crisis can occur at any age and any time to Christians as well as non-Christians. Some men seem to hit a crisis every month when they pay the bills. Others hit a crisis after about seven years of marriage or when they have a milestone birthday like forty or fifty.

A specific event like the loss of a job may trigger an emotional crisis, or it may come gradually over time as a man sees himself growing older without having realized his dreams. Sometimes the entrance of an attractive, available woman in the work environment makes a man question his priorities.

A client named Paul is typical of men entering a crisis. He saw routine settling over his life when he turned fifty. The desires he had for extraordinary success were evaporating. A vague sense of uneasiness settled over him.

At this point some men go into a mild depression that can be brief or may deepen until professional help is needed. Some men try to be a kid again. Don't get me wrong — not all men who buy motorcycles do so because they're undergoing emotional turmoil, but some do. I've seen professional men decide to grow their hair ponytail length. Others start exercising their bodies because that waistline that stayed trim without any effort is starting to look more and more like their dad's.

The most frightening and dangerous midlife crisis occurs when a husband seeks another woman to add excitement to his life and nurture his ego. I wish this never happened, but it does. I advise wives to take practical steps to keep their husband's love like urging him to participate in a weekly Intimacy Reviver. It's like keeping the house boarded up against a hurricane because a hurricane is what divorce is like for the rejected party. Many women have said they would have rather died than have gone through this pain.

Married men face temptations to leave their family responsibilities for other women or for the single life. Some even experiment with homosexuality for the happiness they're not finding in traditional family life. Your husband has a free will and can choose to sin or not to sin. You may do all the right things as a wife and still end up in divorce court. But, of course, you want to make sure you haven't unknowingly contributed to infidelity.

Often during a husband's crisis his wife becomes bitter and angry with him, which only justifies her husband thinking she's a nag. How could he ever have married her? He was too young and immature. His new girlfriend never yells; she keeps telling him how great he is. The wife mustn't try to turn the children against their father and make his attention toward them less.

Typically men in crisis have never known a vital, exciting Christian life. God's Word that gives men a right understanding of their personal dignity and their need to lead a godly family. Family life is being attacked vigorously by the ungodly in society.

Sometimes it's the wife who wants to leave the marriage. Wives need to get help to make their marriage as good as possible. No human relationship is ever perfect, but marriage is a commitment made before God until death. God honors men and women for keeping commitments. Your children will call you blessed for staying with their fathers and helping their fathers remain part of their lives.

Abuse is another issue. Men abuse their wives for many reasons, although alcohol and other drugs are often involved. In some cases, wives are also a contributing factor to the cycle of violence. With her words a woman can devastate a man emotionally. Not every case of wife abuse starts this way, don't get me wrong, but I've seen too many not to mention it. Wives must guard both their mouths and actions.

🖉 *Exploring Scripture*

What does Proverbs 14:1 say about a wise woman? "The wise woman builds her house, but the foolish pulls it down with her hands."

- In what ways have you built your house?

- In what ways might you be pulling it down with your own hands? Psalm 141:3 says, "Set a guard, O LORD, over my mouth; keep watch over the door of my lips."

- How can you use your mouth to build up your husband and marriage?

- Are there any other areas where you need to make sure the Lord is guarding your mouth?

📖 *Taking Action*

If your husband has an affair, go to God before you go to a lawyer. Pray and listen to God — not your family, or friends. Fighting to save your husband from throwing away your marriage will be like riding a bucking bronco — he'll try to buck you off, but hang on. How? Think of him as sick. You wouldn't abandon him if he had cancer. Your husband is spiritually sick. If he had a healthy relationship with God, your husband wouldn't be succumbing to temptation outside his marriage.

Usually you're not the problem. Don't let his criticism of you make you respond in kind. Show him extra signs of your love. Work on your anger with God and with a friend or counselor who doesn't believe in divorce and will help you move into a state of forgiveness. This is crucial if there's to be a future reconciliation, but also critical for your spiritual health.

If your husband shares his feelings readily, be his sounding block, a safe place where he can talk out his successes and his disappointments. If your husband is on the quiet side, be his frequent companion. Be an encouragement to him.

Let your husband know you still love him and want his affection back. Be tender and kind. But don't act desperate and don't submit to physical abuse. That will only lower his respect for you. Wait and pray and be willing to take your husband back in forgiveness. This can work, but it's probably the hardest thing you'll ever do.

Believe what God says about the sanctity and indissolubility of marriage to be willing to surrender false pride and righteous anger. If your husband still insists on leaving, let him go, knowing he may yet come back.

If your husband returns and is reconciled to God and you, your marriage will be enriched as well as saved. Your relationship will be incredible because your husband will personally have experienced the love of God the Father, Jesus, and the Holy Spirit through you.

Remember when you were dating and you couldn't wait to be with him? And you spent time thinking about what you were going to say to one another? Make that part of your married life too. Make sure you don't put your children before your husband. Kids will usually clamor for attention and take all that you're willing to give. Set limits like saying, "It's nine o'clock; Dad and I need for you to go to your room and read, study, or chat on the phone with a friend. This is our private time to talk or watch TV together or go out for a walk."

You can help your husband survive crises by making him feel special in little and big ways.

Make his favorite meal or make a big deal of going to his favorite restaurant sometimes. When my kids were little and I was at home with them, we straightened up the house before Dad came home and everyone met him at the door to make his homecoming seem special. Maybe your husband gets home first and does this for you. Tell him that you appreciate what he does for the family.

Prayer

Lord, I know life isn't always easy for my husband. Teach me daily how to show him love and help him in the rough places. Teach me patience and tenderness when I speak to him. Help me always remember he is a precious gift from You.

THIRTY-ONE
Focusing on God

Y ou can call it prayer, meditation, whatever word you choose, but what does it take to get your head and your heart focused on God? I've asked lots of women this question. Their answers may help you find new ways to give more attention to God in your everyday lives.

Kathy walks every morning and holds a silent conversation with the Lord. Often she uses an alphabet game to stimulate her thoughts. Kathy chooses any letter, like "K" for example, and thinks of words related to God that begin with that letter (or she goes through the alphabet in order). When she came to "Z" I asked what she thought. Her words are zenith, the highest point; zoom, God goes right to the heart; and zigzag, God works in indirect ways.

Caryl goes out to jog and listens to a praise music tape to get her mind and heart elevated above her surroundings.

Terry likes to do something with her hands, like gardening, while she prays. It helps her stay focused. She makes sure she doesn't become more involved in the process of what she's doing than thinking about God.

Connie framed pictures with Scripture verses for wall decorations in her home. She likes to sit in her favorite chair and let her thoughts dwell on Jesus as she looks at them. Like an art museum displays paintings, Connie uses Scripture displays.

My friend Angela needs to read something and uses the written words as a bridge to cross over into her own deeper thought processes.

Pat thrives on hearing how God has helped others. She never misses her two weekly sharing groups with some Christian friends because that strengthens her relationship with God and her dependence on Him too.

Each of these women is refreshed as she experiences God in her own unique way. Find the way that most directly ministers to you personally. Do you respond better through your eyes, your ears, or your hands? Throughout the day you're involved in using all three senses, but which helps you best to direct your thoughts to God?

Whatever it takes, find it and repeat it. Build these opportunities for focusing on God into your everyday life, so that it's natural to spend time thinking on Him.

Both visual and auditory reminders help me. When I decorate, I choose things to remind me of God. For example, I selected a pattern of three geometric shapes on my floor tile to prod my thoughts of the Father, Son, and Holy Spirit.

My house happens to be laid out in the shape of a cross. I often flip on the tape recorder preset to my favorite music. It sets my frame of mind for prayer and becomes an emotional transition.

The goal is to be God-focused in everything you do, but that takes practice. At first be content with simply extending the time you set aside to specifically focus on Him.

📖 Exploring Scripture

Read Joshua 4. Symbols were an important tool God used so that His message would not be forgotten. Can you find a scriptural example of a symbol like stones being used in the Old Testament as reminders?

📖 Taking Action

During your prayer time this week, experiment with a "focusing on God" activity involving seeing or hearing. Which sense best helps you to concentrate on your Lord?

Prayer

Surround me with Your presence, Lord, so I see You everywhere. Thank You for art and music that fill me with sights and sounds of You and keep my mind on Your thoughts and Your ways.

THIRTY-TWO

Leading Others to Christ

May the light of Christ shine in your life and lead others to Him — what a lovely thought. I count it my greatest delight to know Christ and lead someone to Him. Nothing is as satisfying as knowing I've helped someone else to the joy of this incredible relationship.

If you want to lead others to Christ and realize it's also God's command, you may still have hesitations. The most common concerns women express are:

- "I'm frightened at the thought of the awesome responsibility. What if I mess up? This person might be lost forever."

Not true. God can use you, but He does not depend on you alone to accomplish His purpose. You may be the person who gets someone ready. Or you may simply get a person thinking or asking questions. Even if you confuse or disturb people it can lead to their seeking answers elsewhere.

- "I hate to bring up a controversial subject."

You may be afraid you'll be ridiculed. Nobody likes that feeling. You sense that talking about Christ is risky because God isn't everyday conversation in the culture. Yes, it's more comfortable to stay in the background and not risk somebody's disapproval. That didn't bother the early disciples and shouldn't bother us.

- "I don't know enough to counter any objections a nonbeliever may have."

You probably can't answer every person's questions to his or her complete satisfaction. In John 16:8 Jesus said this is the work of the Holy Spirit. "And when He has come, He will convict the world of sin, and of righteousness, and of judgment." It isn't your job to convict people of their need of Christ; the Holy Spirit does. Simply focus on Jesus Christ, His Gospel, and the Holy Spirit because these are the sources of change. The Gospel " ...is the power of God to salvation for everyone who believes." Romans 1:16. You simply give information and ask for reactions like "What do you think?"

- "I'm sensitive to personal rejection if my friend doesn't want to believe."

Remember they're not rejecting you, but Christ. You can point out why others should believe the Christian faith, yet some will still choose not to believe. If you receive a hostile reaction to your efforts, remember that may be the work of Satan who doesn't want this person to know Christ. He can deal with rejection better than you can. Many people who later received Christ often share how someone "annoyed" them with their polite persistence.

- "Should I intrude with my own beliefs? What right do I have to discuss something this personal with another individual?"

Overcome this hesitation by thinking of the alternative. Do you believe hell is real? What would you do to keep a person from destruction for eternity? If you could reach out your hands right now to keep them from physical danger, would you? If you can save them from eternal spiritual and physical agony, won't you try?

- "What do I say, and how do I say it?"

This is where you rely on your study, your experience, and God's power. Acts 1:8 is wonderful encouragement for witnessing. "But you shall receive power when the Holy Spirit has come upon you; and you shall be witnesses to Me in Jerusalem, and in all Judea and Samaria, and to the ends of the earth."

📕 Exploring Scripture

Everybody's got questions and you have answers in Scripture. I like to use 2 Corinthians 5:14-15, 17:

"For the love of Christ compels us, because we judge thus: that if One died for all, then all died; and He died for all, that those who live should live no longer for themselves, but for Him who died for them and rose again..."

"Therefore, if anyone is in Christ, he is a new creation; old things have passed away; behold, all things have become new." In a sense Paul wrote a guidebook in his letters that might be called How a Christian Leads Others to Christ. Paul said to follow his example modeled on the teachings of Jesus.

📖 Taking Action

Sharing your faith isn't a task you perform but a privilege that comes naturally as you live and move about. It's also unpredictable and exciting.

The key elements in testifying for Christ are telling what Jesus did for you on the cross and relating how Christ has changed your life. The Bible can teach a nonbeliever every significant truth needed to live and grow in Christ.

I've been blessed to lead people to Christ, young and old. They've accepted Christ in situations as varied as flying in an airplane, riding in a taxi, or lying on a deathbed.

Think of the world imaginatively as God's garden. Christians all assume different roles in the garden from time to time. Sometimes I'm the flower soaking up the sun, and that's all I can do. Sometimes I provide nutrients for the soil. Now and then I become the soil, like peat for a new plant until it's big and strong enough to be planted outside. Sometimes I'm the gardener fertilizing plants to strengthen their stems and roots. Occasionally I get to revive a Christian flower that's almost dead. And I go through seasons where I drop seeds and multiply! God's garden becomes ever more gorgeous.

- How have other people encouraged your growth?

- What role(s) have you played thus far — set a new plant in peat, nurtured a new bud, an open flower, a little straggly plant in need of fertilizer, the person who fertilizes the soil for others?

- How can you better equip yourself to lead others to Christ?

Prayer

Lord, I love bringing others into Your garden for eternity. I love working in Your garden, tending Your plants, in whatever role You give me. Thank You for the privilege.

⁊⌾⌇ T H I R T Y - T H R E E ⌇⌾⁊
Enhancing Sexuality

A book for women wouldn't be complete without discussing sexuality. Sexual intimacy gives a woman and her husband elation and connection not offered by any other circumstance of life. It's one of God's precious gifts.

In marriage counseling I've seen the pain that comes from not understanding the value of a healthy sexual relationship. In counseling I still have to convince women the value of frequent (at least weekly) sex. You can be sure sex is extraordinarily important to the majority of men. Lustful temptations aimed especially at men are everywhere. I'd estimate well over fifty percent of all husbands deal with regular temptations toward lust. When sex is freely alluded to in the actions, words, and dressing habits of people around us and acted out in television, movies, and advertising, it's a constant challenge to guard thoughts and actions against lustful temptations.

Most Christian men and women handle these temptations well, despite the fact that the sex drive is strong. In counseling women, I encourage them to make sure that their husbands are loved sexually and they continue to find ways to have fun with their husbands in and out of bed. Sexual unfulfillment is a fertile ground for Satan's work, and many wives, without knowing it, help Satan.

The lack of marital sexual intimacy is a problem in Christian culture today. The biggest causes aren't surprising —women preoccupied with work outside the home. Both men and women are exhausted after busy workdays and easily succumb to late-night TV. How can you enhance sexual love in marriage today? Here are some tips.

- If possible, cut back on hours at work.

A woman's energy can be drained by the demands of her job outside the home added to her household responsibilities. When a working mom with children finally falls into bed at night, she wants to be left alone — with no more requests on her from anyone. Often she's simply not interested in anything physical.

- Don't become your husband's "mother."

Carol's husband was proud of her authoritative role at work and the way she managed the children. But he didn't appreciate being bossed, corrected, or ridiculed by her. I helped Carol readjust the way she related to her husband to improve their sex life. No healthy male wants to have sex with his "mother." A woman can help her husband become a lover again by finding things about him to sincerely praise and brag on him!

- Openly encourage emotional intimacy with your husband.

Husbands need to know it's important to their wives not to feel used but to feel treasured. Before becoming physically intimate, a wife can ask her husband what he most loved about her that day. His words can create the emotional intimacy she needs to proceed. I suggest regular use of my Emotional Intimacy Reviver as well.

- Reframe old, negative pictures into positive ones.

Christian women can be highly moral and fully sexual. Even if sexual abuse existed during childhood, or sexual indiscretion during dating, women can have enjoyable sex with their husbands. I use a technique called "reframing" to help people with this issue. That means putting a different mental picture frame around an old print to make it suitable for now. The past was another time, another place. Women need to feel the pain, talk it through with someone they can trust, let go of the pain. Perhaps they need to fully accept the forgiveness of Christ for their past. Then determine not to let the past frame the new picture of life now.

- Enjoy the therapeutic aspects of sex.

Sex has many benefits, too! Sex enhances the immune system, reduces chronic pain by stimulating the immune system, and reduces stress through its natural sedative properties. Sex is perhaps the best preventive and healing medicine there is!

Your sexual activities are a personal topic. I suggest keeping the sexual relationship between you and your husband a private matter. Your sex life is one of the areas in which openness with outsiders is not appropriate.

For various reasons, it may be that you don't enjoy sex and may need to go to a counselor of your same sex to discuss deeper causes. It's best for women to avoid discussing sexuality issues with their pastor or even a professional male counselor.

Remind yourself why you fell in love with your husband. Praise and admire him and you'll find him responding in the same way to you. You get what you give. But be aware if you don't have a sexual interest in your man, it's highly possible someone else will and you're leaving him vulnerable.

What can you do to enhance your sexual relationship? Try these tips.

1. Remind yourself that sex is God's gift to you for physical joy. You can enjoy sex even if you've been raped, abused, or taught that it's a forbidden act. Focus on sex as God's plan, His design for you as a woman.

2. Plan for sexual dates with your husband. Slip away to the bathroom, a walk-in closet, or lock the door of your room and tell your children not to disturb you for a half hour.

3. Be creatively romantic. Don't wait until bedtime to hug and kiss. Women often complain that their husbands aren't romantic enough, but they've stopped holding hands, hanging onto his arm. Sit on his lap occasionally. Reach out and hold his hand when you're walking side by side. If you think your husband isn't still flattered by your sweet words and your physical attention, ask him. You'll be surprised.

4. Discuss sex freely with your husband. Look at him; admire him. Remind him that you still find him very sexually attractive. Yes, tummy and all. Someone else will if you don't. Sadly, some men are attracted to adultery because their wives seldom affirmed their sexuality or verbally or physically express their enjoyment of their husband's body.

5. If one of you must travel in your work, try to keep it minimal. Plan special farewells and return celebrations.

6. If your efforts don't get the response you'd like remember, there are men who could care less about sex. Some have been

sexually wounded and are afraid of sexual intimacy. If that's your husband, encourage him to seek help from your pastor or a respected Christian counselor.

7. Break the routine of your married life. Meet for lunch or go out for coffee and dessert at night. On these mini-dates use an activity I call an IR — Intimacy Reviver — that will promote your emotional intimacy, the rich soil for physical love:

- Discuss your moment closest to God. (God is the source of all love.)

- Share the moment this past week you felt closest to one another.

- Tell one other when you were proudest of your spouse.

- Describe the nicest thing each of you did for your spouse that week.

- Speak only in positives, allow no negative comments.

You're involved in activities during the week that draw you and your husband apart. For one hour draw back together like a rubber band returning to its original shape. How does the Intimacy Reviver work? You make each other happy when you share a proud moment and affirm each other.

🕮 Exploring Scripture

In Proverbs 5:15-23. What are the instructions regarding sex?

Notice enjoying your spouse comes before the warnings about engaging in an adulterous affair.

If you are sharing the pleasures of sexual intimacy with your spouse, running to anyone else's arms is unnecessary. Remember, God sees all.

Be satisfied with your own mate at all times! Let your head and your heart stay busy planning ways to enjoy intimate times with your husband, and you won't get into trouble.

I suggest not being like a woman I'll call Karene. She didn't withhold sex but may as well have. Her reluctance was obvious. She didn't realize how demeaning that was to her husband although she was aware of the words in 1Corinthians 7:4, "The wife's body does not belong to her alone but also to her husband. In the same way, the husband's body does not belong to him alone but also to his wife." (NIV) What a difference when she added love and affection to what she'd considered an obligation.

🕮 Taking Action

- Many wonderful books and tapes have suggestions for showing physical love. Listen to these tapes together at home, and discuss what you hear. Remember, romance starts at breakfast and remind your husband it works both ways.

- What else can you do to encourage sexual intimacy in your marriage?

- Encourage your husband to find as much joy in satisfying you as himself. Don't be shy about telling him what you would like and experimenting. Find satisfaction in pleasing him, too.

Prayer

Lord, every day I want to look at my husband as Your gift to me. Help me to cherish him and love him as You planned for us. Show me see how I can please him sexually and stay close to him as both a lover and a friend.

🔊 THIRTY-FOUR 🔊
Guarding Your Church

*A*s I counsel clients within the church and work with pastors of various denominations I often hear stories of dissension over doctrines and ministries within the church. This strife can occur when a few people begin to advocate a certain way of doing things and prod other church members to follow them until everyone is forced to take sides.

Dissension ultimately destroys the strength of the unified church. The issues that divide can be basic doctrinal tenets or concern with a particular behavior. Just last week I heard of a church conflict when a missionary came back from Africa on sabbatical and began moving exuberantly in their church during services as the worshipers do in Africa. Those opposed felt so strongly against this (they considered it dancing) that they chose to leave the church when the pastor didn't see fit to confront the missionary.

In contrast we read in Acts 15:28-29 the early apostles were sensitive to avoid splits over subjects like the circumcision of the Gentiles. Paul said, "For it has seemed right to the Holy Spirit and to us to lay no further burden upon you except what is absolutely essential, namely, that you avoid what has been sacrificed to idols, tasting blood, eating the meat of what has been strangled, and sexual immorality. Keep yourselves clear of these things and you will make good progress."

(PHILLIPS).

Such tender concern! Such loving acceptance! We are all called to this. God will not tolerate hypocrisy among His people. Is your church focusing more on reaching sinners or promoting doctrinal tenets? Keep straight what's truly important and what's minor. Hate the sin and welcome the sinner.

Jesus accepted the cross without yelling, criticizing, or complaining about the lousy sinners who made His death necessary. Instead He made the most compassionate statement ever spoken, "Father, forgive them, they do not know what they do" (Luke 23:34). Do we truly believe we are to forgive like this? When people sin, do they know what they do? In that moment of action, they made a wrong choice. But do they know what consequences of that act they bring upon themselves and their families from the decision?

False righteousness made Jesus furious. He spoke out strongly against those whitened sepulchers who acted pure on the outside. Jesus saw into hearts and proclaimed there's nobody, not a man or woman, who has never sinned so open up your church doors as well as your arms. Embrace those who are dealing with sin and tell them about the love and acceptance of Jesus.

Guard your church. Part of the church Jesus cleansed has fallen into rigid righteousness again. I know that's true - I've counseled divorced people who have felt unaccepted by their churches. Some churches never allow them in a position of ministry again.

I've heard painful stories from individuals with AIDS who receive more love and compassion from the gay community than they do from people in church. We need a balance between hating evil and loving people. Loving always comes first. Let's not become hypocrites.

Jesus warned devout religious people of His day about preaching love but becoming obsessed with "doctrinal position." When someone sins and repents, do your church members act as if the sin is buried in the depths of the ocean where Jesus puts it?

Sometimes rigid righteousness is a disguise for fear, which gets in the way of love. What do ministers to the sick and dying like Mother Teresa do with their fears? Did the good Samaritan have to overcome fear that the robbers would return? Or that this guy attacked by robbers he helped might end up dependent on him for months? The Samaritan ignored such thoughts and ministered. Oh the sweetness of love. Once you minister to hurting lives, the joy permanently erases fear and selfishness. In that instant you know it's true what Jesus says, "You're doing it for me." (Matt. 25:40).

I once had poison oak and looked awful. I can't begin to express the pain I felt when people avoided me and wouldn't come near, let alone touch me. I could read it in the way they'd sidle away and avert their eyes. It was humiliating. I remember that when I minister to others now.

Pray for God's protection and love; take wise precautions but get involved. You can't let your churches die because members are more concerned with finding others who share their ideology than with sharing the love of Christ with hurting people.

📖 *Exploring Scripture*

Philippians 2:3: "Let nothing be done through selfish ambition or conceit but in lowliness of mind let each esteem others better than himself." If everyone in the church body practiced this principle, we would not have dissension in the church.

📖 *Taking Action*

- Do the words Jesus used for the church people of His day apply to your church? What does your church need to do to show more love to the outside world?

- What can you do to love your fellow church member as Jesus commanded?

The Christian classic *In His Steps* by Charles Sheldon talks about a church community that made a commitment to make every decision as Christ would for a specified period of time. The experiment changed their lives. Would your church be willing to try this experiment? For further application, read *The Body* by Chuck Colson.

Prayer

Heavenly Father, I long to love others as You love them, to see people as You see them. Help me become a person who strengthens my church with love, acceptance, and prayer for both the members and others who come to worship with us.

THIRTY-FIVE
Balancing Effortlessly

*A*s a child, did you ever try walking along a beam as you swayed from one side to the other? You probably had to swing your arms rapidly to pull back to the middle, and then regained your balance until suddenly you started to slip again.

Being a wife, mother, and a working woman is also a challenging balancing act. I've spent decades trying to do the best I can balancing each role. At moments I failed miserably and at other times I've succeeded by God's grace. Balancing is a continual process requiring sorting priorities and wise choice-making every day.

Considering three questions can help you make good choices as you face the challenges of each new day.

- Are you an Anti-Stuff-Person or a Stuff-Person?

An Anti-Stuff-Person says if something is still serviceable, I don't need another. An Anti-Stuff-Person needs to balance by updating clothes and personal items because Christ's witness should represent Him well.

A Stuff-Person says more is better and newer is nicer. Stuffers can overdo purchases.

There's nothing wrong with liking and wanting stuff unless it becomes a consuming focus or the "stuff" requires an excessive amount of selection, expense, and maintenance draining your time and attention. Then it throws you off balance.

Colossians 3:1-2 reads: "You have been raised to life with Christ, so set your hearts on the things that are in heaven,

130

where Christ sits on His throne at the right side of the Father. Keep your mind fixed there not on things on earth."

- Are you a social person (extrovert) or an introvert?

If an introvert, spend more time around people. It's God's design that His people show love for one another. If you're a highly social extrovert, being on the run constantly can detract from your rest as well as your work. Find time to be alone with God.

- Do you love change or resist it?

Whatever your feelings about change, it will come. Life is like a kaleidoscope of constantly moving pictures and colors. Whenever a circumstance in your life changes - you get a new boss, your children start a new school year, your children are on vacation for the summer, your father needs extra care, you move – you'll need to rebalance. All these changes require new decisions about the use of your time and energy.

Too much change too quickly can be unsettling. Psychological stress tests evaluate the number of recent changes in your life. Given a choice, make major changes slowly or keep them to a minimum.

Find your place of peace and balance in the Lord by spending time with Him. Your relationship with Jesus will enable you to enjoy life whatever is going on around you. When God touches your life, He gives you a craving for balance and unrest when you get off balance. If you let him, He'll reorder all your priorities.

Myra had trouble balancing. She prayed, "Show me where to focus my energy and time, Lord. In every area where I have a choice, guide me into Your best for me at the moment." Before taking on something extra, Myra learned to first evaluate her present responsibilities. Only if she was enjoying enough quiet time with God and meeting the needs of her husband and family did she consider adding another activity to her life. Myra made sure she wasn't neglecting these highest priorities.

God taught me about balancing my priorities through the cancer of our son. Before David became sick I was involved in college teaching and completing my doctoral degree. I thought this was extremely important and rewarding. I needed to eliminate these activities to meet my son's needs during his frequent hospitalizations and treatments. I never missed my former activities and I wasn't as indispensable as I thought! Replacements took over and performed well.

📖 Exploring Scripture

The thirty-one chapters in the book of Proverbs have practical instruction for balancing the activities of life. Try reading one chapter each day to correspond with the day of the month. For example read Chapter 9 on the ninth of every month. Highlight every Proverb that applies to your day. Proverbs covers these areas:

- self-righteousness versus hatred of evil
- wisdom versus foolishness
- generosity versus stinginess
- laziness versus diligence.
- order versus chaos

📖 *Taking Action*

- What tends to throw you off kilter?

- When you sense you're off-balance, how do you get realigned?

Prayer

Lord, Your Word is clear. Time with You is my first priority, and my family is second priority. May I weigh the importance of every other commitment in the light of Your Word and daily keep a steady, balance.

THIRTY-SIX

Being Christ's Body

J oan works two jobs, keeps her home immaculate, and enjoys close contact with her two adult sons. She takes "being Christ" to the people in her life seriously and ministers to women she works with through notes, birthday parties for single parents, and planned social outings. She and her husband have loaned them furniture and helped with childcare and household moves. They welcome houseguests frequently, even entertaining parents of their friends. Joan has had recurring health problems, but instead of feeling sorry for herself, she continues to care for others.

Is Joan overly energetic? She doesn't appear to be, nor does she ever seem to be in a hurry. She has simply found ways to use her talents for others in need. Not many of us could keep up with Joan, but we can all find ways to be helpful to friends in need.

The most powerful thing for a friend going through a difficult time is to pray for the person daily. Then stay in touch, make the call, stop by. Forget about the "I don't want to intrude" myth that permeates modern society. If your friend wants to be left alone, your friend can tell you. Even if that's true, your friend will be glad you offered to be available. During an intense crisis, don't let more than a few days go by without contacting your friend. If it's a long-term problem, don't let more than a week or two go by. Encourage your friend to continue her typical schedule. It's easy to drift into a feeling of hopelessness and despair when going through a tough time. Following a normal routine in waking and sleeping and other activities is therapeutic even if you don't feel like it.

If you have been through a similar problem, share pointers you learned, especially biblical principles applicable to the situation that aided you. You're in an excellent position to help. Help your friend reason through to well-considered personal decisions. Feelings of fear and insecurity can entice her to grab at any solution offered. As you hear your friend's concerns, never downplay the dilemma or your friend's concerns about it. It's insulting to minimize what a person's going through.

Be honest. Be dependable. If you say you'll do something for a person, whatever it is — a visit, an errand, a phone call — do it. This isn't a time when a person can handle even small disappointments well. If listening to your friend isn't enough or the issue is very complex, by all means encourage her to speak to a pastor or counselor. Don't make arrangements without asking first. A person in crisis already feels helpless and needs a sense of control over life.

A friend who's hurting may neglect her appearance. Take her shopping, ask if you may accompany her for a haircut, gift her with a manicure, try to help whatever the need may be. This kind of concern can lift someone's spirit immeasurably. Above all, don't expect anything in return. When you have a need, your friend may not even be sensitive enough to see it. Perhaps your friend's own emotions are still too raw from her problem.

Three warnings:

1. Don't be critical of women who don't participate in Christian service you believe they could do. Everyone is given different gifts. Within the church as well as without, be ready to praise and compliment others. Stay away from the strife-mongers. I know of instances of grown sons and daughters who no longer attend church because they saw the pain their parents experienced over unkind words spoken by other church members. As you focus fully on knowing Christ more deeply, meeting your family responsibilities, and being Christ's body to others, you won't have time to judge anyone else.

2. Some acts of kindness may require time away from your family. Your family always comes first. Their needs must not be neglected while you care for others. Your own family mustn't develop a spirit of bitterness. Helping out at a homeless shelter or food pantry is wonderful, but never at the expense of personal time with Christ or the needs of your family. Your caring for others will develop a greater spirit of helpfulness and compassion in your husband and children as long as you don't overdo your service beyond what is pleasing to God and thoughtful of your family (yes, this can happen).

3. From time to time, check your motives. Make sure you don't get addicted to personal accolades from others. Your family needs you but usually won't be showering praise like outsiders might.

📖 Exploring Scripture

1 Corinthians 12:13-14 "For by one Spirit we were all baptized into one body —whether Jews or Greeks, whether slaves or free — and have all been made to drink into one Spirit. [We could add whether rich or poor, brown, black or white, attractive or unattractive.] For in fact the body is not one member but many."

What is the scriptural basis for your connection with others?

"Therefore, as the elect of God, holy and beloved, put on tender mercies, kindness, humility, meekness, longsuffering; But above all these things put on love, which is the bond of perfection.

And let the peace of God rule in your hearts, to the which also you were called in one body; and be thankful" (Col. 3:12, 14-15).

📖 Taking Action

- Relate a time when a friend helped you through a crisis. What assistance did you find most comforting?

- Which of the helps listed above do you feel most comfortable providing for others?

- What do you need to do for someone in need right now that you've been putting off?

Prayer

Heavenly Father, many need love and care. You know those who could best be helped by the attention I can give. I want to be available. Open my eyes to see these needs and respond as You would have me.

≈≈≈ T H I R T Y - S E V E N ≈≈≈
Aging with Grace

*E*ver wonder what life will be like when your youthful looks are gone? Perhaps you're already in the group called "senior." Back in high school and college being a "senior" was viewed as a good thing. "Senior" loses its status as age advances and is often the source of jokes. You can't change the attitude of culture toward aging, but you can change your own attitude.

My mother, almost eighty, doesn't want to be called a "senior citizen." She, like many people, finds the idea of growing old scary. Insecurities, like fear of poor health and concern about sufficient finances, often arise.

Five basic psychological needs remain the same at any age.

- To be in a relationship based on love.

Without a special regard from someone, social hostility can develop. Jenna wasn't receiving love after she lost her family, so she gave love and did good for people around her who didn't expect it. Soon they began to reciprocate and love her in a wholesome way.

- To maintain a measure of security.

Understanding the life, death, and resurrection of Jesus is the greatest security you can have, for without this you can ever experience complete security in this life.

- To find an opportunity for ongoing creative expression(s) in your work or your home.

Ann moved to a condo and left the gardening she loved because her husband was tired of keeping up with the grass and his pride wouldn't let him hire a yard service. Ann developed severe arthritis and seldom left her bed because she'd lost her favorite creative outlet. Keep finding enjoyable ways to be creative. When my mom became housebound, she worked with needles and yarn.

- To be appreciated by someone.

Mary, a seventy-year-old capable waitress, quit her job where she felt loved by her customers and retired with her husband to Arkansas. She died within the year. Often a part time job or volunteer service keeps a person feeling useful and purpose-filled.

- To stay actively involved in life.

Simple things like a trip to the store or a fun conversation with an interesting person can brighten your daily life. Kay moved in with her children and spent her time home alone while they were at work. She didn't drive and never reached out to friends through senior citizen groups. She became nervous, fearful, and forgetful. Stay engaged with others in some way.

Ellen, a "senior" client of mine, had three facelifts, which haven't lasted. She hates the idea of growing old. Why do some women waste time trying to hide the fact that they're getting older? Aging is natural, inevitable, and irreversible. The skin of older women is beautiful like the shine of soft chintz.

I gave advice to Ellen who's concerned about aging. Keep your hair nicely styled and attend to your grooming. But most important of all, keep your life purposeful. Stay focused spiritually through God the Father, Son, and Holy Spirit are the source of your vitality. Stay in charge of your life as much as you can even if you are in an assisted-living environment. Whenever you lose old friends because they move away or die, seek a new friendship to fill the void.

Don't become critical of the world because the pace is too fast or blame the young because they are too busy to visit you. Explore recent changes in the culture, like technology, with an open mind. Look for activities you can enjoy at a pace that's pleasant for you.

Continue to use your gifts. I've read accounts of people diagnosed with degenerative diseases and senility who experienced miracle 'cures' when they got involved in exciting new activities. If you truly can't get around well, you can still have a powerful prayer ministry. Pray for God to show you individuals who need your daily prayers.

Avoid dawdling, move purposefully. Never stop exercising or eating well. You're always God's temple. Rest more if you need to, but spend some time each day with other people, including children. It will keep you feeling vitally involved in this adventure called life. When it's time to move into eternity, welcome the new phasc of life.

📖 Exploring Scripture

Psalm 103:5 "God satisfies your mouth with good things, so that your youth is renewed like the eagle's."

- What does God do for His people all throughout life?

Hebrews 3:14 "For we continue to share in all that Christ has for us so long as we steadily maintain until the end the trust with which we began" (PHILLIPS).

What is Christ's promise as you near the end of your life? What are you to maintain until the end?

God's Word says He will give you the desires of your heart. (Psalm 37:4). He doesn't add until you're fifty or sixty or eighty-five. Your job is to stay tuned in to the Holy Spirit and find what those desires should be and then live in joyful expectation of seeing God work no matter how old you are.

📖 *Taking Action*

Whatever age you are, remember to have a cheerful, kindly disposition in old age, you need to work on developing these traits now. The major problem older people have is not their physical limitations but the psychological limitations they create for themselves by poor thought control.

- Which of the tips for aging with grace do you need to incorporate into your life?

- Think of a recent situation where you reacted with grumbling, crabbiness, or worry.

Describe how the same situation could have been handled with acceptance, determination, and cheerfulness.

Prayer

Dear Lord, we're all on the same path — time is passing. I want to enjoy every moment of this precious life You've given and live by Your standards. Keep me strong, Lord, and looking forward to each step of the way.

THIRTY-EIGHT

Resolving Conflicts

C onflict resolution is not a power struggle where one side wins, but a method for solving disagreements so that both sides are pleased with the outcome. I always teach conflict resolution skills as part of my marriage and family counseling.

Kerry caused great damage to her husband's self-esteem and their marital relationship by refusing to listen when she didn't agree with him. She never really attempted to work through their differences in a calm, loving manner. Anytime a serious problem arose she threatened divorce. One day her husband shocked her. He responded, "Go ahead, I don't care any more."

Conflicts arise anytime two people with different, temperaments, values and experience try to get along — especially in a close relationship. But there are healthy and unhealthy ways to deal with these conflicts. Continually threatening divorce as Kerry did is not the healthy way.

Before you start to try to resolve a conflict, pray for God to bring you to a mutually agreeable resolution. Then follow these guidelines:

1. Attempt to resolve a conflict quickly unless you're too upset or your temper is totally out of control. Then wait a little while. Schedule a time to sit down to talk though the issue and resolve it. A disagreement can be like a rolling snowball - it keeps growing until you stop it.

2. Before expressing a complaint, express your genuine appreciation about a positive behavior of your husband or

child. Always avoid derogatory phrases like "That was a dumb thing to do."

3. Use specific, clear words to describe any behavior you didn't like.

4. Restate how your partner responds to make sure you understand the other point of view. Don't assume you know how your spouse is thinking or feeling — ask.

5. Stay focused on one issue at a time. Don't get sidetracked. Avoid bringing up past behaviors that have been forgiven.

6. Brainstorm for how this situation might have been handled differently.

7. Eliminate words like "You never" or "You always" or "I'll never be able to" or "You should" or "You shouldn't." They divide rather than unite.

8. If the other person won't listen or tends to yell, hold an object and pass it back and forth. Maybe use a spoon if you're in a restaurant or a golf ball at home. Only the person holding the object can speak, then passes the object to the other person. This provides each person an opportunity to speak calmly without being interrupted - a simple, effective listening technique. Another suggestion is writing a letter; use word pictures like "I feel like a plant that never gets watered."

9. Leave other relatives' traits and personality issues out of your discussion. If your spouse doesn't stick to the immediate conflict, make sure you do.

10. If after you've both had your say and you're no closer to a resolution, pray together (or silently if the other person refuses). Wait quietly for God to work. Do whatever He suggests. Sometimes His answer may be to keep still.

📖 Exploring Scripture

Read Matthew 26:31-35. How did Jesus handle disagreements? In the Gospels we read He patiently sat down and told His disciples they had drawn the wrong conclusion and explained what they needed to do. Jesus had several conflicts with Peter. He told Peter, "Peter, you are going to deny me when I'm arrested and you're confused about what to do next."

Peter said, "I won't deny my ties with you; I'll be loyal." But Jesus knew better. After the Resurrection, Jesus gently reminded Peter. Jesus didn't give up on Peter; He forgave Peter when he didn't measure up. He gave Peter lots of chances. That's what you and I need too — give spouses lots of chances.

📖 Taking Action

Set your phone to record yourself the next time you want to discuss a behavior of your husband you don't like. Evaluate how to handle the situation in light of the conflict resolution guidelines above.

- Did you express genuine appreciation? What positive things did you say?

- Did you allow your husband (or the other party) to explain their side of the issue, and did you listen?

Keep these resolution guidelines on the side of the refrigerator or posted in a cabinet where you can reread them from time to time.

Prayer

Lord, I want to get along with people in a healthy way, face honestly any problems between us and resolve them as quickly and kindly as possible. I need patience, courage and wisdom from Your Holy Spirit.

THIRTY-NINE

Breaking Negative Patterns

O ften clients come into my office after struggling with a negative habit a long time. They know these thought patterns or behaviors are unpleasant, annoying, and possibly sinful, but feel powerless to stop.

Consider these examples of typical negative patterns. Sue is in bondage to procrastination and disorder. Jane has a compulsive need to have perfect order in her home. She gets depressed over any mess and yells at her children constantly. Ann always looks picture-perfect when she goes somewhere and gets compliments on her appearance, but leaves her home looking like it's been burglarized.

Karen's in bondage as a never-say-no do-gooder. She gets pats on the back for being helpful which she loves. This hides her negative patterns of low self-esteem and a sense of being purposeless.

For another woman a negative pattern might be the tendency to gossip by disguising it as "sharing prayer concerns." As she prays, instead of feeling compassion, she feels a tinge of superiority that she doesn't have this problem.

A negative pattern can become a major spiritual struggle if allowed to continue. It's like when I got poison oak. First the rash was minor and contained on one area of my skin. The next thing I knew it had entered my bloodstream and began to spread throughout my body. The itching became torture. No topical ointment helped until I treated the deeper infection within my blood with steroids and antihistamines.

I find roots for women's present responses and negative patterns in their past experiences. This doesn't excuse them only explains. Perhaps a parent never expressed love, or there was too much pressure to excel coupled with lack of success in school. Explanations alone aren't enough to solve the problem. Once individuals recognize their negative patterns, they must avoid fixating on the reasons for them ad nauseam over months or years.

Clients need to decide both that they want to be free from these patterns and use God's help to end destructive habits holding them in bondage. Entire books have been written on the subject of right thinking, but there's not enough power in positive thinking or intellectual knowledge to be set free. The power comes from God.

The main principles needed to live as God intended free from any bondage or negative pattern come straight from God's Word. If you've been clinging to a destructive pattern, these next steps can help you change.

- Ask God to help you pattern your habits after those of Jesus. Study His Word to learn how you ought to think and act. Then put into practice the truths you read; it's not enough to pray and then wait for God to change you! God gives you the responsibility to respond to His Word with your actions.

- Name any negative pattern(s) you recognize in yourself. Identify the reason you've been drawn into this negative pattern, write it down too. If you're unsure, ask a friend whose confidentiality you trust help you find the source of the bondage.

- Replace a negative pattern with a positive pattern. For example, replace impatience with compassion. You are changed by renewing your mind - you don't simply remove a negative attitude or behavior by suppressing it.

Transform yourself, little by little, by thinking and acting the opposite of your former way.

Begin to think and act as if you have this habit under control. This is what Paul calls "setting your mind" in Colossians 3. He also talks about "putting to death" (these old patterns won't die on their own, you need to kill them), "ridding yourselves," and "putting on" the good and the positive. Yes, think and act that way, even if briefly at first, until the new thoughts and behaviors become natural.

📖 Exploring Scripture

Study and memorize Psalm 16:5-11 (NIV) to break negative thought patterns and fix your mind on the good patterns God has for you. With all the positives He gives, why stay stuck in negatives?

LORD, you have assigned me my portion and my cup; you have made my lot secure.
The boundary lines have fallen for me in pleasant places; surely I have a delightful inheritance.
I will praise the LORD, who counsels me, Even at night my heart instructs me.
I have set the LORD always before me.

Because He is at my right hand, I will not be shaken.

Therefore my heart is glad and my tongue rejoices, my body recite this Psalm every night before falling asleep. If you're tempted to doubt that change is possible, meditate on 2 Corinthians 5:17. "If anyone is in Christ, he is a new creation, old things have passed away; behold, all things have become new."lso like to memorize Philippians 4:8.

📖 *Taking Action*

- What negative patterns do you allow to control your life?

- Write a description of the positive thought patterns or behaviors you can develop in place of negative ones.

- Ask a prayer partner to pray for you to succeed.

Prayer

Lord, give me wisdom and patience to practice better behaviors and the will to keep at it so I'll be daily transformed more and more into Your image.

🌭⌒ F O R T Y ⌒🍭
Encouraging Communication

W ould you like to have a guest in your home who never stopped talking and insisted on your attention and your husband and children's? And to top it off — the guest taught your children behavior you didn't want them to learn! How long would that person be welcome? Well, if there's a TV in your home, you have this type of guest!

Lorie wanted to improve communication in her family, and she knew TV viewing was preventing normal family conversation. Lorie decided to limit TV time in her home.

One of the greatest blocks to a healthy relationship between children and parents is television.

Children immersed in television simply don't learn to find pleasure in everyday talk. The same can happen if your child or husband spends a lot of time on the computer. TVs and computers are like an addictive drug. They pull the watcher insidiously into dependence. When the screen is off, they feel uncomfortable like something is missing. An extended deprivation of several days causes irritability and moodiness.

Not only does TV promote violence, which you've heard repeatedly (and not enough has been done to eliminate it), but TV actually harms children. I see it in children I counsel. TV makes children passive communicators. They will respond when adults ask them direct questions, but they don't initiate questions and general conversation. In effect, they lose the ability to communicate spontaneously and act bored and sullen in response to life around them. Becoming uninvolved in normal activities, they're ripe for temptations.

Some families remove the TV completely. I'm not totally against TV, but opposed to its taking over as the most powerful "family communicator." I suggest one hour a night maximum is a good rule, except possibly for a sports program which models activity. Withdrawal from excessive TV takes at least six weeks to two months. Be prepared. Some moms tell me, "TV is wonderful when my kids are sick." But remember how, as children, many of us enjoyed the extra attention we received from a parent during illness — being fussed over, playing games with an adult, or being read to. Isn't that better?

I'm for family communication and fun. Establishing good family communication requires attentive planning — it doesn't just happen!

Here are some tips for encouraging family communication:

1. Don't expect strong relationships to simply happen. Take the responsibility for improving your relationship with God, your husband, your children, and the other significant people in your life.

2. Think ahead of conversational starters for family dinnertimes just as you would with adult friends.

3. Take time to play with your children and not simply plan fun activities for them. Keep badminton set up in the yard and swing a racket around after dinner with your family, playboard games, walk the dog together.

4. Ideally find some activities that each of your children enjoy and plan a time for sharing these activities with them.

5. Make silly talk occasionally.

6. Model and teach good listening skills. Slow down, make eye contact, practice listening for "feelings" as well as words.

7. Be especially sensitive to your younger children when an older brother or sister dominates family sharing time. Be alert to younger children's needs when an older child leaves the home for school or marriage. This can be a difficult adjustment period for the child (ren) still at home because the family dynamic changes. You may be experiencing a sense of loss as well, but you'll help yourself by focusing on your family's needs and planning fun times with your child (ren) at home.

8. Follow the "A Little" principle: "A little alone time, a little family time, a little planned time, a little unplanned time, a little TV, a little self-generated entertainment."

🕮 *Exploring Scripture*

What principles does God's Word give for TV and for family communication? First Corinthians 14:40 says, "Let all things be done decently and in order." This great verse on order was originally applied to church meetings but is appropriate for every activity involving Christians.

📖 *Taking Action*

- Which family communication activities listed above might work in your family?

- What can you do this week to promote opportunities for family communication?

Prayer

Heavenly Father, guide me as I plan wholesome family activities for us. I want to create special times that build healthy relationships that last forever.

ꙮ FORTY-ONE ꙮ
Equipping Children

J oanna wanted her live-in twenty-six-year-old daughter to be more independent. She claimed her daughter didn't have skills for living on her own. When Joanna's children were growing up, Joanna admitted she did everything for them. Her children became self-centered from her constantly waiting on them and pleasing them. Mothering and training are positive — smothering and babying are not.

Joanna wanted to compensate for what she lacked during her childhood. As a child she'd never had activities outside school because her parents both worked. She wanted her children to have these "opportunities" so she said yes to whatever they wanted to be involved in. Growing up Joanna hadn't had many friends so she wanted her children to have lots. No time remained for her children to help out at home, so Joanna did everything.

When her children became young adults, their demands intensified, but Joanna no longer had the stamina or desire to keep the pace. I helped Joanna understand the source of her feelings and become secure enough to risk displeasing her adult children and nicely say, "Manage for yourself."

It would have helped immeasurably in their personal development if Joanna had taught her children the skills they needed when they were little starting with small household responsibilities. Chores are wonderful! Teach children to enjoy them! And along the way every child needs to memorize Colossians 3:23, "Whatever you do, do it heartily, as to the Lord and not to men!"

Train your children to use the proper methods to accomplish tasks. How often do you assign a task to our children and expect them to figure out how to do it? And then complain because it wasn't done right. I was guilty of this.

In 1 Chronicles 22:5-11, notice how David made the preparations and laid the groundwork for his son Solomon's success before he gave the command to Solomon to get to work building the temple. Then David prayed for the Lord to help make Solomon successful. He also told his son to carefully observe all the laws of God. He encouraged Solomon to be strong and courageous — not fearful or easily discouraged. David's son Solomon did the work, but David made sure Solomon was equipped. He told him clearly what to do, and had other men available to help him.

Once children are grown, married, and have children, they're physically capable of living on their own. Of course, occasionally they may need help briefly. Emotional and spiritual parenting is a lifelong process. Children don't ever outgrow their need for advisors and encouragers.

✍ Exploring Scripture

Every child needs to be taught about the Lord. In Psalm 22:30 we read, "Posterity will serve him; future generations will be told about the LORD" (NIV).

Ephesians 6:2-3 is the first commandment with a promise attached, "Honor your father and mother . . . that it may go well with you and that you may enjoy long life on earth" (NIV). Prepare your children for success in this world by teaching them to honor the Lord as well as those in authority over them, starting with you.

📖 *Taking Action*

- Are you doing too much on a daily basis for your children?

- What tasks can you hand off to them right now?

- Have you trained your children as well in manners, social customs, and people skills as you have provided academics and sports for them?

When children are overly dependent on their home environment, they sometimes become overly dependent on the school environment when they go off to college (which is why they delay graduating).

- Where do I need to begin preparing my children to become more independent? What responsibilities can I give them now?

- Am I equipping them to deal with life apart from academic skills? List ten practical things your children should be able to do as a teen.

Prayer

Lord, I love my children and enjoy helping them. Help me discern necessary mothering from an unhealthy tendency to keep them dependent on me. May I build both their roots and their wings.

ஃஃ FORTY-TWO ஆஆ
Loving the Corinthians Way

I really thought there must have been a misprint in Scripture when I first read in 1 Corinthians 13:5, "It [love] is not irritable or touchy" (LB). That means love does not take offense! There have been times I've wanted to yell, "Not take offense, but do you know what he or she did to me? Surely this situation is different!" Wrong!

We can easily be offended by people we see often, which is why marriage and other close relationships are a challenge for 1 Corinthians 13-style love.

Yet God expects love to be the norm, and He specified the way to make that happen. He never asks us to do something without giving us the tools and equipment needed to get the task done. Loving without taking offense is imperative in your continuing to love and keep promises and commitments.

I've often failed at this miserably. In the early days of my marriage, before God changed my thinking I used to make mental lists of my husband's offenses to tell a friend once a week. Instead of feeling better after I shared my hurts, I simply fired up my anger. My husband would wonder why I'd come home so annoyed and tense after my evening out.

I met lots of young wives with attitudes similar to mine. Anna was a lovely teenager I met soon after she became a Christian. I lost track of her until she turned twenty-eight and came to me for counseling. Although still very beautiful, Anna was now a nervous woman — her hands shook, her voice was a monotone. Her face had lost its serenity, and her eyes no longer held the glow of joy. What had happened?

156

After visiting with Anna a half hour, I identified her problem. It could be summed up in the words, "Love is not irritable or touchy" from 1 Corinthians 13. Anna had written her own mental book of all the offenses committed against her by her family, her friends, her church, and on and on. Some friends didn't call her enough; somebody else dropped in too often.

Anna couldn't forgive her pastor for his insensitive comments to her husband although she said she'd tried over and over. What she really meant was "I won't forgive him." She considered attending another church because she could no longer get anything from the pastor's sermons. Anna explained to me how upset these people had become when she pointed out how they offended her. "But aren't you supposed to tell people how you feel?" she asked.

In intimate relationships, yes. And if people are committing sin, Scripture has a clear plan for addressing the problem. But if you just don't like something or are slightly inconvenienced, then, no. There's been too much "Let all your feelings hang out" in every area of life imaginable.

The saddest thing of all is that Anna had long ago lost her own joy and her peace by her habit of taking offense. Love must be slow to lose patience, and your model here is God's patience with you. Constructive patience and kindness includes positive words and not expecting or demanding apologies from others who have wronged us. It is God who makes all things right.

Certainly if a Christian is in sin, the problem should be taken up with that individual. But if a person's behavior is simply annoying you, that's your opportunity to practice love and draw on God's grace. Deciding not to get annoyed and practicing silence is best.

So many wedding ceremonies include 1 Corinthians 13, the "Love Chapter," among their Scripture readings, yet few marriages or other relationships follow its mandate for not taking offense. I reread this chapter often and apply it as my sermon to live by.

As hard as your pastoral staff, your business associates, your family, or your friends try, you will at times be offended by what they do, don't do or say. But Jesus loves you, and you must love others. If you struggle in this regard, place this motto where you'll see it often: Love Every Offense Away. Not taking offense sounds hard, but it's for the tough areas like this that God generously pours out His grace — or none of us would succeed!

✒ *Exploring Scripture*

Read 1 Corinthians 13 aloud as if the words were spoken just for you. By far the hardest part of this chapter to live out are verses 5 and 7 (NIV). "[Love] is not rude, it is not self-seeking, it is not easily angered, it keeps no record of wrongs." "It always protects, always trusts, always hopes, always perseveres" (vv. 5, 7 NIV). J. B. Phillips puts love this way: "Love has good manners and does not pursue selfish advantage. It is not touchy. It does not keep account of evil or gloat over the wickedness of other people."

📖 *Taking Action*

- God loves me and forgives me the 1 Corinthians 13 way.

- Where do I need to show my love and forgiveness to others?

On a separate sheet of paper, make a list of all the people who have offended you or are offending you right now. Then tear up the paper and resolve not to dwell on how you've been hurt ever again! Only God's grace makes this difficult act of the will possible. I have clients do this exercise in counseling sessions between husbands and wives. One wife refused to destroy her list. She wanted to keep bringing the subject up again and again. She would not let go of her past hurts, and her counseling sessions proved ineffective.

Prayer

Heavenly Father, my mind is full of offenses and perceived wrongs and this list is very close to me. Parting with my list is like parting with a dear friend — but not a friend — an enemy that keeps Your love from flowing freely through me to others. By an act of my will I tear up my mental list and choose to forgive.

FORTY-THREE

Hearing God

"It's not that I have any doubt that God can speak to me, but I'm not important enough that He would speak to me. Besides, how could I hear His words without being concerned I might distort them?" Kara, a young career woman, asked me during our counseling session.

"Isn't that an insult to the communicative ability of God who wants to be understood?" I responded. "Don't you think He can make His message clear? Wouldn't He create you with spiritual antenna to hear Him?"

Eventually Kara realized she had dulled her relationship with God with a meaningless routine of rote prayers. God's mercies are new every morning, but she wasn't experiencing them. She needed a reminder that His communication is always available and signifies His mercy and kindness.

The real difficulty in hearing God is a six-letter word, L-I-S-T-E-N. I took a survey of how many people spend five minutes a day listening to God, and my survey found listening is probably the most neglected act of piety.

My husband and I have hectic schedules. We're often running in different directions When I sense myself drawing apart from him — not divulging intimate thoughts because he isn't available or I'm too tired, I make a point of reconnecting. Otherwise he misses out on insights I know he'd like to hear about the children and other matters, and I don't get to hear about the special moments of his days.

God reminded me that that's how He feels when I don't schedule time for Him. I start to feel as well. Yet I know He hasn't broken our connection — I have. I miss out on the encouragement, wisdom and guidance He wants to give me.

God is available to be in creative contact with us throughout the day. He can use other people and even nature to demonstrate His presence.

How do you maximize listening to God?

First by setting aside time, then what? The next requirement is putting your other thoughts aside — your ideas of what God should say. Be prepared for anything.

Here's the sort of thing I may hear: God may urge you to do something or He may want you to do nothing but praise Him. He may show you a principle for someone else you know and guide you to share it in love. He may give you a sense of His awesome love right now even in your human imperfection. This is my favorite kind of communication.

God may lead you to a book or a portion of Scripture that speaks to a need in your life at this moment. He may guide you through a strong impression to a certain course of action. I have heard God in each of these ways at different times.

📖 Exploring Scripture

Look up 1 Samuel 3:10, "Speak, for your servant hears." This was the response of Samuel and many other Scripture giants to God's voice.

Name some people in Scripture whose lives were totally changed by what God revealed to them?

📖 *Taking Action*

- How much listening time do you give God each day, each week?

- Pretend Jesus is sitting in the front seat of the car when you run errands.

- Chat with Him. What is He saying?

You might want to out for coffee and sit alone in a booth. Pretend He's across from you. Talk to Him in your heart. Read a Scripture passage and write down your impressions of what it means for your life right now. Whatever creative type of situation it takes for you to begin to hear God, do it until hearing Him is such a natural joy, you can't bear to miss it!

Prayer

Speak, Lord, I am listening. I am listening through Scripture; I am listening in my heart. I am listening through the voices of my friends and loved ones. I am listening through nature. I am listening for Your voice.

𝕾𝕰~ FORTY-FOUR ~𝕾𝕰
Entertaining God's Way

*T*wo of our best friends, Tom and Pat, have brought more than a hundred people to a relationship with Christ by inviting strangers they meet to dinner at their home. They have a modest home, and if Pat doesn't have time to clean and polish as she'd like, she keeps the lights dim and burns a lot of candles.

If Jesus were walking through her town, Pat would be ready to say, "Stop over and spend the night." She could also easily add, "I'll have some friends in to meet you." Is this pleasing to God or what?

Through His frequent contact with people, Jesus stressed the importance of spending time with others. After all, how can you love our neighbor if you're locked in your house each night staring at TV or isolated with your family?

Luke 14 could be called the "party chapter" in Scripture. Read it aloud and notice how often a dinner party or a gathering of friends is mentioned. Jesus gives two guidelines in this chapter for you when you entertain.

1. When you give a luncheon or dinner party, watch that you don't just invite friends of the same social status. Invite those who cannot repay your hospitality.

2. When we're the one invited, be a humble guest.

From Jesus' use of the word when, it's obvious Jesus expects us to be entertaining regularly. His message is "get out and party." The old Girl Scout song is still a great ditty, "Make new friends, but keep the old, some are silver and the others gold." (author unknown).

In the days of Jesus a host first invited a group of guests, then gave a second invitation after everything was prepared. There was always room for one or a few more, but a group took planning. You aren't supposed to imitate exactly the customs of Jesus' day; obviously, our culture is different, but you can extract the essence of its lessons for today.

Examine your mind-set toward entertaining. Do you see yourself in any of these examples?

When Carla was a child, she used to hate family parties because she came from an alcoholic background. Every time guests were invited, Carla did all the prep work beforehand, all the serving during, and the clean up afterwards which exhausted her. Then the evening would inevitably end in a screaming match between her parents. When Carla married, her husband liked to have his family over for dinner often, and insisted that the meal have two meats, two vegetables, rolls, a couple jellos, an assortment of relishes, and several desserts. It never occurred to him to help.

After counseling, Carla said, "I'm balancing my husband's wishes with what I can handle comfortably. I used to identify easily with Martha in Scripture. But my husband began to help me out in the kitchen. Now he understands we can serve a pot of chili, toss a salad, and loaves of French bread. He began to understand this dinner was not the only meal our guests would eat all week and it didn't have to be super fancy. Far more important - we could enjoy more time to visit."

Little by little Carla learned to stay calm and relaxed as she prepares for company yet be filled with excitement. She keeps the meal streamlined and enjoys her dinner parties as much as her guests do.

Many women prefer to entertain friends in restaurants because it's hard to get their houses in order for entertaining or they don't think their decor is nice enough. At times the convenience of meeting in a restaurant is the only way busy people can get together, but pleasant as restaurant food can be, the ambiance of sharing of your personal home is lost entertaining out.

Don't let pride get tangled up with enjoying your guests. Entertaining is not show-off time. That makes all the fun and relaxation disappear. I've been down that street in the early years of my marriage, and it's not worth the frazzled nerves and marathon productions I used to make of a simple thing like company for dinner. Who did I exalt by having everything "just so"? Do you fit anywhere in these examples?

Here's an easy way to entertain a group. I picked up this idea when I was waiting to check out at the grocery store in Wisconsin last weekend. I watched as the lady in front of me emptied her cart on the counter. She pulled out bags of prepared salads (the kind that are prewashed and include a bag of dressing and croutons and "dump and serve" are the directions), then she lifted out pre-sliced, pre-buttered loaves of garlic bread, a couple jars of spaghetti sauce, and spaghetti noodles.

She'd have to spend twenty minutes watching the noodles and sticking bread in the oven. I figured she easily could feed about twenty people for about twenty-five dollars. Yes, that's more money than if she made everything herself, but compared to a restaurant tab, it's not high.
Obvious, she wouldn't be impressing her guests with her gourmet cooking skills, but the point is she was having a group in and being hospitable.

You can be ready to entertain Jesus and His disciples or your family and friends at any moment, too!

📖 Exploring Scripture

Read the story of Martha and Mary's entertaining. Don't you feel sorry for Martha with all that work to do and Mary wasn't helping, even though Jesus said Mary chose the best part? Didn't Jesus realize how tough it was to feed a crowd?

Before you answer, read Luke 10:40, "Martha was encumbered about much serving" (KJV). "Cumber" — what an interesting word — it sounds so heavy and laborious, and that's what it means. Phillips' translation reads, "But Martha was worried about her elaborate preparations." Jesus knew very well that Martha had "over care in service." She needed to be corrected for becoming "cumbered" with entertaining.

📖 Taking Action

- Make a list of the people you'd like to entertain in the next several months.

- Set a couple dinner dates for the next several weeks. Plan a basic, simple menu for dinner.

- Write the menu on a 3x5 card along with a shopping list on the back. Finish all household projects and heavy cleaning the week previous. Ask your husband and children for special household help if you need it.

Try to have everything done at least an hour before the guests are due. Walk through the rooms where your guests will be and pray they'll be blessed by their time in your home. Sit for a few moments to relax yourself.

Prayerfully invite Jesus in advance to every party you have. Prepare some spiritual discussion to serve along with every meal. As you set the table, pray for your guests to be blessed by being in your home. Check Reader's Digest or Guideposts for some inspirational stories you can share. Or talk about a current event and its moral implications. As the conversation lulls or as a related subject comes up, share the inspirational thoughts you've prepared.

Have fun! Jesus did and He wants you to also. A note for further application in your family: Your family needs to be entertained as specially as guests occasionally. Dine in a place in your house where you don't usually eat. Set up a card table in the living room and serve dinner there. How about eating on the porch? Amazing how a change of scene slows children down.

Prepare some family-sharing questions like: What would you like to do that you've never done before? What do you like most about each person here? Set the table extra special, maybe use place cards of poetry or Scripture verses for the children's names and let them guess which verse is theirs.

Prayer

My home is open, Lord. Fill it with the people You want here. Help me to think clearly and creatively as I prepare; keep me calm. May I focus on being a blessing and not on creating a masterpiece.

FORTY-FIVE

Staying Culturally Involved

*T*he social culture and political culture are continually in a state of change. You adjust to it, up to a point. Whenever absolute Christian values get mixed up in the bombardment of the world's philosophies, be wise and vocal about speaking out and taking action with gentleness and courage.

If we're to help others, we must stay involved with the world about us and not withdraw from it. Sadly as a brand-new Christian, I seriously considered aborting our fourth child when I had a surprise pregnancy. A life-threatening physical condition with my third pregnancy could easily recur. Also, my husband and I had a major RH blood incompatibility problem and we were medically advised not to have more children. Another baby would need a dangerous total blood transfusion at birth - a great risk. Plus, who would raise our three other children if I died during the delivery of our fourth child.

In this situation I had to come to terms with what I believed about God's will and his power over each life. The culture around me made abortion seem a logical choice. Several Christian people had studied both sides of the issue and listened to my concerns. Without condemning me for considering abortion and without denying it was the "world's" valid option, these friends helped me sort through my priorities in light of God's truth. Discussing both sides of the abortion issue with these intelligent, caring Christians helped us make the right decision. If they'd just preached at me, I might have been turned off.

I decided to trust God and have the baby, even if it meant dying or caring for a handicapped child. God would empower me. During this time, many of my deep theological questions were resolved. Amazingly our son Daniel was delivered by caesarean section and neither of us had complications, praise God!

God's forgiveness is always available to women, non-Christian and Christian, who chose abortion and regretted it later. I've been privileged to counsel several women working through this experience in an atmosphere of God's love.

Abortion is just one of many social and political issues needing vigilance. Christian women must be vigilant in guarding against abuses. Women need to keep the public schools teaching the basics and leaving the social issues to families. The entertainment industry needs vigilant women to guard against the immorality it produces. Our Lord wants men and women keeping track of wise local decision-making on events concerning your community, your city, and your schools.

Some Christian women aren't aware of the rights they have in the public domain. Several Christian legal organizations like the American Center for Law and Justice help people being persecuted on religious grounds.

"Letters to the Editor" are widely read in most newspapers and are a valuable resource for Christian women to express their views. Here are some guidelines:

1. Identify an issue in the news
2. Define the issue for the reader who may or may not have seen the original story
3. Apply biblical truth to the issue
4. Reinforce it with a quote from Scripture
5. Write with respect and courtesy

📖 Exploring Scripture

Any confusion about whether or not to be involved actively in the culture around you should end when you study the gentle but firm Esther in Scripture who developed both her wisdom and her feminine attractiveness. She used tact and careful planning in approaching the government of her day and saving the Jewish people from annihilation.

In the New Testament, the activist Priscilla together with her husband, Aquila, risked social pressure to support the apostles of Jesus. Acts 18:26 says, "So he [Apollos] began to speak boldly in the synagogue. When Aquila and Priscilla heard him, they took him aside and explained to him the way of God more accurately." (Acts 18:1-3). Priscilla and Aquila started a church in their home (1 Corinthians 16:19).

📖 Taking Action

Stay alert. Read the papers or a weekly news magazine. Listen to talk radio. Understand BOTH sides of issues, but don't just read and listen. Respond. One call, tweet, email or letter every week can become fifty-two a year. When you call or write: first politely describe what you appreciated and would like continued or expanded, and then second, describe what concerns you and what you'd like done.

Call the library and ask the reference librarian to help you find the address you need to send the letter. As you accumulate a collection of addresses of TV stations, radio shows, and members of Congress, tape them inside a kitchen cabinet and share them with other women. Have your older children write letters too - a quick after-dinner family activity you can supervise along with kitchen clean up. It builds good habits in your children, and children's letters are noticed.

Gather women together to monitor issues and pray. Visit your movie theater, your school board, your local bookshop. State pleasantly and firmly what your expectations are regarding morality. Become an advocate for short-distance, personalized government. Be patient. Don't expect quick results, and don't quit!

Prayer

Lord, forgive me of the sin of standing by and letting others do the job of speaking Your truth in my town, schools, and country. Keep me alert about current events and willing to make my voice heard in calls, email and letters. Keep me sensitive to minister to friends and acquaintances who may need an informed word of wisdom from me.

FORTY-SIX
Enduring Tests and Trials

S cripture tells us that there are times when God either allows or sends afflictions for the ultimate benefit of His children. No one likes to hear this. We all think it's great when we don't have to strain to meet challenges in life, when we can enjoy blissful periods without major relational flare-ups, or job or school problems, and when everyone in the family is healthy and happy!

Suddenly something goes wrong, and the sweet period end. It's time to regroup and figure out how to survive the trials that have popped into your life.

Sometimes tests and trials come from Satan. Remember Ezra, the man who committed to serving God with his whole life? He was involved in rebuilding the temple of the Lord - a good thing, to be sure. Ezra 4:4, "Then the peoples around them set out to discourage the people of Judah and make them afraid to go on building. They hired counselors to work against them and frustrate their plans during the entire reign of Cyrus king of Persia and down to the reign of Darius king of Persia" (NIV). Ezra had to endure trials that came from his peers and outsiders hired to thwart him.

God allows trials to accomplish His purposes in your lives. Some Christians don't like this idea, but if we deny a God who tests His people, we twist God's character to make Him into our image of how we'd like God to act.

Remember Abraham and Isaac in Genesis 22? Talk about a test of obedience — lay your son on the altar and offer him as sacrifice. But by then Abraham had learned that he could trust God no matter what! And remember it was the

Holy Spirit who urged Jesus to go into the desert to be tempted by the Devil. Yes, God knew Satan would test Jesus there! God uses all things, even tests and trials, for our good.

A fifty-year-old client of mine, Sally, experienced a difficult time when her husband lost his career-track job. His ego drooped dangerously low. He was moody and depressed and began to speak belligerently to Sally and the children. He refused to get a low-paying job saying something in his field would turn up any day. Sally had put up with his attitude several months, but was getting fed up with his doing nothing. She came to see me prepared to offer Frank an ultimatum: get any job and stop making everyone in the household miserable. Both Sally and Frank were scared.

Frank still needed time to deal emotionally with his job loss. Certainly change was in order. Not for a minute would I suggest that Sally shouldn't strive to help Frank improve his behavior, but the harshness of her demands could have pushed him to seek divorce. When I suggested God might be testing Sally's ability to show compassion and build her husband's esteem, Sally shook her head in disbelief. She was a woman of prayer who loved Jesus more than anything, but she couldn't believe God would ever send her and her husband this trial.

Like many tenderhearted women, Sally viewed God as an indulgent parent who protected her from every pain. Sally became angry when I pointed out God sometimes allows trials to test or mature her. When this trial came, Sally preferred to blame Satan or the sinful nature of men and women. She began to change her perspective and found peace. Nothing like testing to show a person's level of obedience and commitment.

Whatever the source of your trials today, God gives sufficient grace and strength to get through. Expect trials in this life, but refuse to be overwhelmed by them. God may be teaching and training you.

📖 *Exploring Scripture*

According to Psalm 119:71, "It was good for me to be afflicted so that I might learn your decrees" (NIV), and James 1:2, "My brethren, count it all joy when you fall into various trials, knowing that the testing of your faith produces patience." What benefits can come from affliction?

Read Jeremiah 35:1-19 about the Recabites, some interesting people God tested. In this passage God told His prophet Jeremiah to give wine to the Recabites despite the fact they had a commitment to the founder of their religious order not to drink. Wisely the Recabites refused the wine. The Lord told Jeremiah to go to the men of Judah and compare the faithfulness of the Recabites with the Israelites' disobedience to the important commands of God.

📖 *Taking Action*

When our son developed cancer and we were praying for his healing, he was hit by a drunk driver and his leg was shattered along with other more minor bruises. In looking back I believe Satan may have been trying to destroy our confidence in God, and God may have been testing our commitment to maintain our faith in Him when He allowed the second calamity.

- Describe a time when you feel God may have been testing your faith through a trial.

- Help your children endure affliction and God's testing in their lives by telling them how you've benefited from some of the trials of your past.

Prayer

Lord, I long to grow and mature through the difficult times of my life. I long to experience them in the light of Your overall purposes for me, learning what I need to learn and being mightily strengthened further for service.

FORTY-SEVEN

Training Children

*T*hink about what you're teaching your child. You have a powerful influence over the behavior of your children. Don't believe you "can't do a thing." You can set consistent standards for your children and firmly follow-through on your standards every day. God's principles in Scripture will guide you in doing a great job with your kids training them physically, spiritually, emotionally, and intellectually.

Discipline is challenging, and incredibly essential and rewarding.

Three important principles are basic in nurturing and training:

1. Motive
2. Positive expectations
3. Opportunity

These are proactive tools, not reactive, they require planning in advance.

Motive. It's OK to reward your child's good behavior in a tangible way. Some parents feel children should experience inner satisfaction from trying their best and doing the right thing.

This is true, but spoken rewards and gifts are okay too. A child as well as an adult likes praise and appropriate material rewards. Maybe your disapproval is expressed frequently through grounding or time outs, but how often do you express your approval? A good rule is to use three comments of praise for every correction.

Drew and Jack, ages six and seven, couldn't remember to turn the bathroom lights off. The boys weren't trying to be disobedient but needed a reminder that would work. I counted out twenty-five pennies for each and put them on the dining room table. I said they could keep the pennies after their visit, but every time they left a light on after they left a room, I'd take back a penny. This is using a reward, a concrete symbol, to teach a household rule — and it works.

Positive expectations

Expect the best of your children. Research has demonstrated that children tend to live up to the expectations parents or teachers have for them. Tell your children in advance what behavior you expect from them in a situation. "I know you're going to give a nice welcome you give to your cousins" or "Remember your good manners at the restaurant" or "I'm expecting you to do a good job cleaning your room."

Expect to find joy in parenthood. You'll never regret using your time and energy training your precious children. It's the best investment you'll ever make.

Opportunity

Be mindful of every developmental stage of your child to be sure your behavioral expectations are appropriate and your little ones have the ability to do what you ask. I have to smile when I see a parent trying to reason with a four-year-old. The capability to think abstractly isn't developed until about age seven. Until then, children need to respond because you expect it.

Keep your children's environment as simple and organized as possible. Have lots of shelves for their toys. Toy boxes don't work as well for maintaining order. Alternate toys by packing some away and switch out a "fresh" batch every month. Have pegs for pajamas and clothes.

Well-trained children are an incredible joy to you and to others. When your children are young, you relive parts of your own childhood. When they get older, they expand your world with their friends and activities, and when they're adults, they'll give you interesting new perspectives.

When your children have children, you'll have a chance to impact your grandchildren's lives too. Then when you're old, the little children that you made time for, and spent your resources on, may be the ones who care for you. This is the cycle of giving and receiving through the years.

✆ Exploring Scripture

What has God commanded in Proverbs 22:6? "Train up a child in the way he is to go, and when he is old he will not depart from it." If you nurture your children well and guide them in right thinking, choices, and actions, it will stick with them.

Proverbs 12:1 says, "Whoever loves instruction loves knowledge, but he who hates correction is stupid." Remind your children discipline is valuable and a sign of your love.

📖 Taking Action

- Children are to be a blessing and a joy! What changes in the behavior of your children need to happen for them to be blessings and joys?

- What changes do you need to make in yourself to help your children change?

- How can you use positive expectations, approval, and rewards to motivate your children to make these changes?

Prayer

Thank You, Lord, for my precious children. Give me Your wisdom to train them effectively.

FORTY-EIGHT

Bonding Brothers and Sisters

You want to instill sibling love minus rivalry in your children. Two boys, aged five and two, were lost in a national forest for twenty-four hours. The older brother took care of his little brother until they were found. He said he was scared but didn't want to show it so his brother wouldn't cry. What a picture of love between two so very young boys! On the other hand, I've also seen brothers and sisters expressing deep hatred for one another.

Brothers and sisters, left to their own devices, can be competitive and critical of one another. Not only do they often fail to encourage one another in sports or creative work, they actually discourage one another with put-down remarks.

Children in the same family often tease one another. This teasing can purely fun or it can be harsh and cruel if it hits vulnerable points of a brother or sister and is a disguise for meanness. It can simply be a way to get Mom or Dad's attention or a symptom of an underlying problem of insecurity. Sometimes kids are just bored and fall into troublesome behaviors because their energies are not positively directed elsewhere.

In our home I recall a few knock-down-drag-out battles. The children competed against one another in sports and games, but overall kept it fun. They learned love, acceptance, and compromise. Then, when our son David needed a bone marrow transplant, each of his sisters and his brother willingly underwent tests to see if they could be the donor.

Tamara, a new bride of five months, was selected as the closest match. I had to live next to University Hospital for two months during David's transplant. David's other sister, Pamela, a senior in college, got special permission to student teach close to home so she could care for her other brother, Dan, our junior-high-age son during my absence. Dan visited David every weekend with games and videos to help make the days of isolation more palatable.

On transplant day, all the children wanted to be present. None of the siblings complained about the disruptions to their lives during David's illness. The statue of a boy carrying his brother on his back with the inscription "He's not heavy, he's my brother" tearfully reminds me of the preciousness of their sibling love.

Yes, your children will disagree occasionally because they have different opinions. Encourage them to talk about their feelings honestly and kindly. Let them know you expect them to be different from each other but also to respect and treasure one another.

You might try these things you can do to encourage healthy bonding among your children.

1. Little children will fight; how you handle it is important. Sometimes it's best to separate them and forbid them to play together for a time, maybe an hour or two. Your children will start to long for each other and be much kinder when they play again. Or you can try sending them to the same room; they must stay there together until they can tell you how they'll solve the problem without fighting next time.

2. Take your children's pictures together often, like on the first day of school every year; take family pictures on holidays and during vacations. Stress that this picture shows them with their brother or sister, and they need to take care of each other. Teach family respect. Say, "You're a Rolfs (or a Smith), and it's a privilege to be part of our family."

3. Once a week, ideally on Sunday, make it family day, a time to enjoy one another. Plan activities for all your children to participate in. Enlist your husband's support. If you have more time, do the planning, but make sure your husband has an active role to play. Yes, some of your children may grumble, but say, "Sorry, this is the plan; you have to join us." Have dinner in the dining room and make a celebration of it. Play board games in teams to make it fair (like Monopoly or Sherlock Holmes Baker Street where you try to solve a mystery). Enjoy one another's company. Perhaps sleep together on quilts in front of the fireplace, like a pseudo camping trip at home.

4. Insist your children listen to one another and value one another's ideas. Remind them that no one starts out perfect. Set firm rules that they cannot damage or destroy each other's work or possessions.

5. Plan activities where your children have to work as a team. Give them chores to share. Let them divide up who should do what. Encourage them to help one another with projects.

6. Of course you'll never foster sibling rivalry by favoring one child over another.

📖 Exploring Scripture

Look up Mark 1:16-19, 29. Peter and Andrew were brothers and buddies. They worked together and lived together and Jesus called the two together. Obviously these men understood Genesis 4:9 where Cain asked God, "Am I my brother's keeper?" They knew the answer was, "Yes!" As rugged outdoorsmen, Peter and Andrew looked out for each other. We never read about Andrew's objecting to the Lord, "Why can't I be the rock upon which You build Your church Jesus?" No whining, "Why Peter and not me?" James and John also were called to follow Jesus together. When their mother, the wife of Zebedee, came to Jesus to ask for good spots on either side of Jesus for her sons in the kingdom, she inquired equally for both of them. No parentally induced sibling rivalry there.

When a problem arises, sit down with your school-age children and discuss these problem-solving steps:

1. Review the goals - to get along with a brother and sister with love, fairness, and kindness; to avoid envy, argument, and unhealthy competition.

2. Review the circumstances that led to the problem.

3. Have them discuss how they might react differently in the future to avoid the problem.

4. Think of a disagreement as a challenge to be met and resolved. Moms and Dads, don't get caught up in the argument.

One more thing — Jesus calls us His brothers and sisters. Isn't that an awesome privilege!

📖 *Taking Action*

- What have you already done successfully to bond your children and reduce sibling rivalry?

- Which of the suggestions given above might work in your home?

- What do you need to do to improve the relationships with your own grown brothers and sisters?

Prayer

Heavenly Father, good relationships among siblings don't just happen. I need to teach our children to respect one other and work out their differences. Help me see their squabbles as opportunities for growth.

Facing the Future

E lsie, age fifty-five, admitted she was a driven women, scurrying around, always looking ahead fearfully. She'd become depressed when her nest emptied. As she aged she started to fear that she might lose her husband and his emotional and financial support. She became paralyzed by concern over the future and lost her delight in the present. She worked long hours and was too harried to do more than survive. She couldn't eliminate her job, because she feared having enough money for retirement or medical problems.

When you look to the future you can foresee changes ahead — both positive and negative ones. If you have children and they leave home for good, it can be a traumatic change. It isn't easy to grow older and not be able physically to do the things you once did. The future does involve losses. I encourage clients to admit this, but with preparation, transitions come more smoothly.

Throwing out anchors into other areas of your life along the way helps. You need strong interests in several areas to replace the interests of your younger years. Continue to make new friends. Many women develop powerful ministries in the later years of their lives when they are free from family responsibilities.

What do you believe about retirement? The whole retirement concept can be a trap. It can create unnatural fears and mess up your life right now. Does God really mean for you to retire? You never heard about Eve or Sarah retiring. Consider Caleb in his old age. Caleb pleased God because he refused to allow fear of death to govern his decisions. He put his trust in God, and God said they could enter the Promised Land.

Caleb knew the danger; he had personally scouted the fortified cities and the land and saw the giants they'd have to overcome. He stated, "We are well able to overcome." (Num. 13:30).

How could he be so confident? He refused to fear. He had faith in the power of God to help him deal with any problem. God rewarded Caleb for his faith and trust.

How about Job? Did Job worry about the future even after he lost all that he had? No way! Did he ever retire? What were his latter days, the typical retirement period, like? Job 42:12, 16-17 says, "Now the LORD blessed the latter days of Job more than his beginning; for he had fourteen thousand sheep, six thousand camels, one thousand yoke of oxen, and one thousand female donkeys... After this Job lived one hundred and forty years, and saw his children and grandchildren for four generations. So Job died, old and full of days." Did he keep busy? Even overseeing the people who cared for all that livestock was full-time work.

Death is a reality in your future and mine. Accepting the inevitability of death is wise. Recognizing death as a fact will help you focus on living well. Death is not to be feared, nor are the unpredictable circumstances of life reason for fear.

Too many women live in a nagging fear regarding the future while one of their biggest fears should be dying without having really lived. Women shouldn't be willing to put up with unbiblical situations in their lives instead of working to change them.

You can face the future bravely by living a full, rich life every day. Every stage of life has its upside and its downside. Christ came to give peace and perspective despite anything that might happen in the future.

✒ Exploring Scripture

Psalm 91:15 says, "He shall call upon Me, and I will answer him; I will be with him in trouble, I will deliver him and honor him."

What does God promise to do if trouble comes?

Some excellent verses for meditation as you face the future without fear are:

- First Corinthians 2:9: "But as it is written [in Isaiah 64:4]: 'Eye has not seen, nor ear heard, nor have entered into the heart of man the things which God has prepared for those who love Him.'"

- Psalm 16:11: "You will show me the path of life; in Your presence is fullness of joy; at Your right hand are pleasures forevermore."

📖 Taking Action

- Be honest. What concerns you most about the future?

- Complete this prayer: "Dear Lord, help me to relax in You concerning..."

- What areas of your life do you still need to give totally to God?

Prayer

Thank You that I can trust in You both now and in the future — that the path I am on will never be without Your love and presence.

ஜ்~ FIFTY ~ஜ்
Worshiping God

W orship is an intimate expression of adoring love. Scripture says that God inhabits, lives in the worship and praises of His people. God desires worship as your Creator.

Why should you worship? Out of awe for God's creation? For His amazing ways? Recently, through the study of genetics and DNA, scientists have acknowledged the facts of Genesis that all mankind came from one man and one woman. The first human was made of clay just as Genesis described.

God made you and the beautiful world around you. But that's not all. He sent His Son to atone when you mess up. If you're a mom, think about what a blessing this is.

Atonement was and is a big deal. Which of your children would you sacrifice if their life could save the whole world? God offered Jesus Who willingly died for the world after enduring a horrid process of incredible suffering.

After this agony, Jesus rose from the dead. Witnesses, thousands who watched His crucifixion, saw Him after He arose. If you don't believe this, you may as well deny the whole record of history. More evidence exists for the life, death, and resurrection of Christ than for a great deal of what children learn in history class today.

Obviously, worship is in order, but how and where? In public or private, at church or at home, at work, all throughout your days, are you aware of the living God with you? You probably do a fair amount of talking each day both aloud and in your head. How much of it is to God? How would you like it if someone acted as if you weren't present at all? God is honored through your awareness of Him.

Many forms of worship exist – through words of praise and song. Yet in some churches beautiful songs are sung about God but not to Him. Have you ever raised your hands as you pray? Are you concerned about looking dumb? God wouldn't think so. At first it may feel awkward, but soon it can become a natural expression of lifting your mind and heart to God. Try it at home or sit in the back row of church on Sunday if you're worried others will watch. They may decide to try it, too.

Moses held his hands up to bring victory in battle. Jesus stretched His hand forth to heal. Lifting is symbolic of dedicating your hands and your entire self to God. In Isaiah 6:1-4 the prophet Isaiah saw the Lord high and raised up. Because of that vision he was changed permanently. God became the focus of his life. I wonder how many times Isaiah, in his private worship, relived those moments in his mind? Is that vision what gave him confidence to go on when the people rejected him and misunderstood his message?

What if you started your worship with the memory of a time when you were aware of God's unmistakable, undeniable real presence in your life? I often use the picture of myself in a hospital chapel surrendering my sick son to God even as I implored Him to save our son's life.

Another time I recall being prayed over in an atmosphere where I felt the presence of God ever so strongly. The person prayed, "Let there be more of God and less of 'you,'" which I took to mean less of my pride, selfishness, and defensiveness, which had been my desire for some time.

After the prayer I lay on the floor flat on my back worshiping God and repeating over and over in awe, "In His presence is the fullness of joy." I've never felt so close to His glory. I wanted to stay there forever, but twenty minutes was all I had. I'll remember them all my life.

You may have had more or less dramatic experiences of God's presence. But think back to when you've known God was there. Afterwards perhaps you said you must have imagined it, but in the moment you knew. Treasure those moments, dwell on them when you start to pray.

You may find it difficult to worship God and enter into His presence because of bad memories from the past popping into your head when your mind is still. A little voice whispers, "Not you, you're not worthy, remember such and such?"

Fight these thoughts. We all have experiences we'd like to forget forever, but God in His wisdom reweaves them in our lives into a prettier fabric than before. Learn to appreciate His designs.

When you close your eyes to pray in church, close your mind to the things of the world. Let your worship be real, not a mere ritual. When you get to heaven, it won't matter if you raised your hands or knelt or lie flat to worship It will be important that you loved God and loved others with all your heart and you weren't afraid to show it. However best you like to worship God, do it. Worship Him because He alone is worthy to be praised. You were created to be in constant relationship with Him.

🕮 Exploring Scripture

In Matthew 2 the Magi worshiped.

- Nothing stood in the way of the Magi's reaching Jesus.

- They thoughtfully planned their gifts in advance.

- When they found Jesus, they were filled with joy.

- They bowed and worshiped Him humbly.

- They presented their gifts.

- It's best not to judge the worship style of others. The traditions of other Christians may be different; it's not how you worship but that you truly worship that matters.

Look up Colossians 2:16: "Therefore do not let anyone judge you by what you eat or drink, or with regard to a religious festival, a New Moon celebration or a Sabbath day" (NIV).

🕮 Taking Action

Give your children opportunities to join in your acts of worship. Plan a special family worship service at home.

Experiment with other forms of worship. Write a song or praise letter to God. Worship Jesus as you load the dishwasher — praise the Lord for the equipment, the soap that you don't have to make yourself, the healthy bodies that ate this food on these dirty dishes. Read how Brother Lawrence in the classic book The Practice of the Presence of God worshiped God in all his daily chores.

Prayer

Lord, may I never forget I was created for fellowship with You and not created to do work for You. I need to practice here on earth what I will be doing in heaven — praising You.

FIFTY-ONE

Being a Grandma

G od expects grandparents to set a good example for grandchildren to follow. Each child is loved unconditionally by God, and often first experiences His love through parents and grandparents. I want mine to remember me as someone who loves the Lord and them wildly.

I'm sure you see the value of being an actively involved grandparent. Scripture is big on lineage- notice the numerous lists of ancestors - because of the incredible impact parents and grandparents have on future generations. You have an intercessory prayer role on your grandchildren's behalf. Every morning my husband and I pray for our grown children's and grandchildren's safety, protection and guidance throughout the day. We pray they'll learn only what's emotionally, physically, and spiritually sound and forget anything not wholesome or worthwhile.

As a grandparent you also have a powerful role as encourager and backup trainer, but be careful not to intrude and assume parenting responsibilities that are not yours. Their primary trainers are parents.

Tips for being a wonderful grandma.

- Never miss an opportunity to demonstrate love, but don't be just a "yes" person to a child. Let your grandchildren know you have expectations for their behavior. Be willing to discipline when you must. Overindulgence is not fair to their parents, plus it undermines consistency especially if there's a contrast between your discipline style and what your grandchildren experience at home.

- In order to be an encourager you need to focus on each child individually.

- You need time to study each child's personality differences, talents, interests, and skills.

- This will help you select books and activities geared to outside interests. Adapt activities to a child's abilities so that you can help foster each child's uniqueness.

- Praise your grandchildren's parents for any good you observe in your grandchildren — polite manners, a kind gesture, a good habit that you see. Your adult children need to hear about their successful parenting victories. It's easy for parents to become discouraged. Who's in a better position to tell them their parenting is working than you? Incidentally, if you haven't told your children about God in their youth or they weren't open to hearing, present the Gospel to them now as adults. They may be more receptive to hearing when they're searching for truth to teach their children.

- Tactfully make parenting suggestions you feel are appropriate. If you think the parents are being too strict or too lenient with one of your grandchildren, say, "Maybe I'm wrong — I know I only observe a small bit of your interactions — but do you think possibly... and make your suggestion?" Be as nonjudgmental and noncritical as you possibly can but do share your thoughts. Always model in front of your adult children healthy parental interactions with your grandchildren.

- Keep alert to your grandchildren's stages. Refresh your memory with books on child development. You've been through it, but you forget, and some things you possibly didn't learn.

- Keep a bin of art materials and age-appropriate toys in your home. Make a special place for books. Be sure the grandchildren always clean up before they go home. Remember, you're trying to instill good habits.

- Have special date or appointment times. If you live close to your grandchildren, each week take one child alone for a special time at your home. Play a game after dinner or plan an outing your grandchild will enjoy. This helps grandpa have time, too, instead of only grandma developing relationships with the grandchildren.

- Do whatever it takes to stay in communication no matter how greatly you're separated by distance. Use letters, postcards, tapes, videos, or e-mail with computer-literate grandchildren. With postal system and technology, it's never been easier to keep a long-distance relationship strong.

"Well done, good and faithful servants" includes grandparenting tasks as well. If children are arrows in the quiver, what are grandchildren — the arrowheads that will penetrate the future?

Exploring Scripture

2 Timothy 1:5: "When I call to remembrance the genuine faith that is in you, which dwelt first in your grandmother Lois and your mother Eunice, and I am persuaded is in you also." Timothy's faith was a result of prayer and Christian training of his mother and grandmother. Wouldn't you like this to be said about you and your grandchildren?

Taking Action

Your number one action is praying for your grandchildren. Write their names on a daily prayer list and keep it by your bed or on your refrigerator (I paste their pictures on it, too). Pray for each child by name often.

If you're a mother, what can you do to involve your children's grandparents more directly in their grandchildren's lives?

Prayer

Thank You, Lord, for my precious grandchildren and for their parents, my dearly loved children. May my prayers and actions bless them and lead them ever closer to You.

FIFTY-TWO

Experiencing Contentment

*F*eelings and circumstances change. I wish each of you could spend time sitting in my counseling chair. You'd hear a woman with a handsome husband say she no longer finds him physically attractive and would like a divorce, or one with an attentive husband complaining her husband always want to know everything she's doing, a woman with a workaholic husband complaining he doesn't make enough money. Some women desire to marry, but the right man doesn't come along. Others marry and wish they hadn't.

The point is that during one period of life, your husband may seem like the most wonderful man in the world; at other times you're sure he's a loser. He may be your greatest joy or your toughest trial. Your husband is never home as much as you'd like then one day he retires and all of a sudden he's around too much. Nothing stays the same, least of all your feelings. Circumstances will never be perfect on earth.

But Jesus Christ is the same yesterday, today, and tomorrow. No matter what is happening in our life, you can experience ten thousand joys in Him if you look to Him for your contentment, your approval, and your deepest pleasure. Contentment is not the same as complacency. You always need to improve what's within your ability to change and develop yourself into the best person you can be.

Some women live with very difficult circumstances. When Cleo was a young woman in her thirties, she used to daydream her drunken, abusive husband would die. He badmouthed her to others even at church, and everyone thought she was the "bad guy" in their marriage who caused him to drink.

Christ comforted her and motivated her to pray for her husband. Cleo did the Christ-like thing. She didn't feel love for her husband, but she knew God did. Christ gave her the peace and contentment she needed to enjoy life despite her circumstances.

Cleo learned to listen to God and live in the minute. She kept focused on Jesus for her esteem instead of trying to justify her actions to others. After thirty-five years of marriage, Cleo's husband joined AA. He became a Christian in reality, not just in word, and started behaving like a tender husband. When he died several years later, Cleo grieved deeply and couldn't imagine life without him. Once again her relationship with God kept her from being disconsolate and gave her the ability to live joyfully.

In contrast, Dana talked constantly about leaving her insensitive and critical husband. Dana was a Christian and wouldn't divorce him, but her home life was miserable. For years she complained to anyone who would listen. Dana said, "I no longer feel love for my husband."

I told Dana, "Treat him as if you love him because you made a vow before God to love him as long as you both shall live, and vows made before God are not to be broken. As you act that way, your feelings may very well change. Even if they don't, you're honoring God by your obedience and He will bless you." I didn't suggest that she hide her feelings, only that she control them.

Dana continued to moan about her unsatisfied emotional goals, household tasks her husband didn't complete, and family needs neglected. Dana's childhood memories of her parents' quarreling made her feel guilty about her griping, but nevertheless she repeated for her children the pattern of family life she'd hated. Needless to say, Dana never experienced contentment in her life. She refused to move past her anger and bitterness.

Each woman has a choice to make — contentment in Christ or dissatisfaction with life. Feelings and behaviors can be brought under control and changed by an act of the will. There's a popular saying that feelings are neither right nor wrong, they simply are. What we do with those feelings can be very right or very wrong.

Because feelings change, it's important to base your life on truth. Don't let your happiness rest on the behavior or words of others. Base your primary happiness and joy on your relationship with Jesus Christ. Basing your joy and happiness on Jesus Christ alone doesn't mean you are to allow yourself to be physically abused. You need to seek professional help to learn how to stop the abuse and preserve your marriage. Contrary to popular psychology, most women should be able to handle verbal abuse without being devastated. Remember the old saying, "Sticks and stones will break my bones, but words will never hurt me"? The Lord can help you hear verbal abuse and maintain healthy self-esteem.

Very often a husband's verbal abuse stems from his own lack of inner security. Certainly this is undesirable, and a wife must pray for her husband's emotional growth. Typically her pleas alone will not motivate him to behave differently, and he needs outside help.

No matter what your situation, it's never impossible or too late to experience contentment. Perhaps you've never been married. Or you've lost your husband through divorce or death, and you're grieving for the past. Soak in the security of the constant things in your life now. The sun rises every day for you. Night settles over each day to refresh you. Sleep gives a new start to each tomorrow. And Christ is present to husband you perfectly whatever your condition.

📖 *Exploring Scripture*

What does Ecclesiastes 3:1-8 say about experiencing contentment in the present? There's a time to have babies and a time to be done, a time for saving and a time for garage sales and moving, a time to be sad and a time to be glad, a time to be patient and a time to speak, a time to build houses and a time to sell, and a time for... whatever is going on in your life right now.

Ask God for the wisdom He promises in James 1:5 for your present situations. Accept what you must, and embrace all that life holds for you that's been allowed by God. Knowing

God's in charge, you can go through the cycles of your life with confidence and contentment.

📖 *Taking Action*

- Describe an example from your own marriage when you've needed to change your feelings so that you could experience contentment in your relationship.

- How can you find greater contentment with God?

- With yourself?

- With your husband?

- With your family?

- With friends and acquaintances?

Prayer

Lord, I can be miserably discontent with everything around me or find my contentment in You regardless of my circumstances. I make the choice. May I be content, not merely passive or indifferent. May I control my feelings, not hide or suppress them. My deepest peace and joy come from You.

Epilogue

*F*ifty-two ways to help you keep your promises and your commitments on your run through life! I hope you feel motivated and encouraged.

It takes a whole lifetime to learn how to run the Christian race well. God gives signposts along the way to keep you going in the right direction and making the right choices.

He also wants you to run at your own speed, your own natural pace, and have fun, and experience joy along the way. I've asked God if there's anything I need to add to this book. I sense He said, "Tell the women I love them, say it again, I love them. I delight in them as they are, while I help them become all they can be. Remind them these ways aren't supposed to be a hard 'To Do' list but fun. Remind women to laugh a lot. Laughter is the music of heaven, and these women are My joy."

About the Author

Dr. Judith Rolfs has written seventeen books on family issues and several inspirational mystery novels including the popular Tommy Smurlee children's fantasy mystery series teaching positive morals. She has a B.A. in Psychology, M.S. and Ph.D. degrees in Counseling and Guidance.

Years of working with parents and children and raising her own four children and grandparenting seven make Dr. Rolfs uniquely qualified to share her knowledge. Her parenting courses and workshops have helped families deal with challenges and led to the development of effective strategies for dealing with issues every family faces.

Judith loves helping women live fantastic, funfilled lives!

EBOOKS AND PRINT BOOKS AVAILABLE ON AMAZON BY DR. JUDITH ROLFS

For Adults

Never Tomorrow, page-turner inspirational mystery novel

Directive 99, futuristic suspense novel

Bullet In The Night, inspirational mystery novel

52 Ways To Keep Your Promises As A Husband and Father

Man in Command, How To Be A Great Husband & Dad

Loving Every Minute, 52 Ways To Live, Laugh & Love As a Woman

Love Always, Mom, A Real Life Miracle Story

Triumphing Over Cancer, A Patient & Caregiver's Manual of Encouragement

Joyful Christmas Reflections

God Thoughts

Secrets of Being A Super Grandparent

For Children

The Adventures of Tommy Smurlee, Mystery fantasy for boys & girls 8-14

Tommy Smurlee and the Missing Statue, Mystery fantasy for boys & girls 8-14

Unforgettable Stories For Kids

Hey, I've Got ADHD, Here's How You Can Help (written from the point of view of a child)

Hey, I've Got Cancer, Here's How You Can Help, (written from the point of view of a child)

Truth for Teens, Answers to Life's Tough Questions

WILL YOU LEAVE A REVIEW?

If you enjoyed this book please leave a review
on the book page at amazon.com.

Visit Dr. Rolfs' website:
www.judithrolfs.com

You may want to check out the companion book for men, *Man In Command, How To Be A Great Husband and Dad*. The Introduction and First Chapter follow.

Man In Command

How To Be A Great Husband and Dad

Dr. Judith and Wayne Rolfs

Copyright 2014
Dr. Judith Rolfs

Dedication

To Chester Vandy and Virgil Rolfs, dads who recognized the importance of family and left a legacy of unconditional love that I'm privileged to pass on.

WHAT READERS HAVE SAID ABOUT MAN IN COMMAND:

MEN ARE RESPONSIBLE for a healthy marriage and happy family. This book can help men fulfill their important biblical responsibilities and avid stress in the family. Dr. Bill Bright, Founder and President of Cru (Crusade for Christ International.)

This is a week-by-week walk in obedience to the Lord Jesus Christ. Discover one new way each week to accomplish His goals for your life!

Table of Contents

INTRODUCTION

The Bible's practical spiritual and emotional lessons can help men in everyday family experiences. Men can model these scriptural principles for their children. Today many men haven't learned these principles and don't know how to live by God's Word. Broken promises and loss of credibility characterize their lives.

Man in Command, How To Be A Great Husband and Dad will help every man be a great husband and dad. The strategies include enjoying and finding satisfaction in these roles. Of course, the 52 ways written here will not create a flawless person—that's God's job. God is the expert, but He has given clear directions and specific principles found in His Word.

God blesses the nation and the men who will courageously live by His Word. If men don't personally guide their children, the powerful forces of the media and peer culture will take over the job. May you commit yourself to be a *Man in Command* — for yourself, your spouse, your children, and for the Lord!

#1 Being An Encourager

Suppose your wife prepares a special meal, but you don't particularly care for it. What if your son strikes out in a baseball game instead of hitting a home run? Are you able to affirm their efforts anyway and help family members feel valued and significant regardless of whether they succeed at tasks or please you in the moment?

Encouragement, men, is the grease that lubricates the wheel bearings of life. The members of your family need your support no matter how well or poorly they perform a task.

How much of an encourager are you? Even though common sense tells you that nagging is wrong, do you tend to harp on some characteristic of your wife or child that irritates you? It's easy to slide into nagging by continually dwelling on minor faults. This deeply injures your wife or child's emotional and spiritual wellbeing.

Of course you need to teach your children a good work ethic and create high personal standards.

Kids should be clean and well groomed to start the day. Children need to be courteous to family as well as friends. These practices are a necessary part of training little ones. Beyond that, however, there are gray areas that are open to choice. You need to avoid nagging about issues of personal preference.

Wayne discovered he was nagging rather than encouraging when he kept reminding our teenage son David that he wasn't weight lifting enough. Once, twice, three times a night, Wayne would ask David if he'd worked with the weights yet. David finally told his dad how much he hated his constant picking and how he'd lost any desire to exercise.

Rather than constantly nagging, it would have been far better for Wayne to pump iron with David and spend the time encouraging him.

The fact is, nagging can't produce the level of perfection we desire in our marriages and in our kids. Constantly noting imperfections leads to discouragement or even despair. It's a sure way to sabotage emotional and spiritual growth.

Often what you perceive to be a fault is merely a personality difference or an interest preference. Your child may not be as outgoing or as driven as you'd like but may be responding appropriately—just differently than you would. For example, some children are naturally more relaxed and slow moving. It does no good for you to prod them to hurry up. In fact, it creates a harmful tension contrary to their innate makeup.

Our youngest child, Dan, moved at a slow pace but always did an excellent job in a reasonable amount of time. Because of his highly organized nature, he planned his work rather than plunging into it haphazardly. Wayne appreciated Dan's work style and encouraged him in his work at his pace. This is the kind of patience and encouragement the heavenly Father models for us.

The key is to identify and praise your wife's and your children's strengths. Your encouragement strengthens the ability of your family members to cope and be productive despite minor human imperfections. Accept their uniqueness. Be very cautious in criticizing minor habits or styles of personality. You want to help them flourish under your encouragement into the people God wants them to be.

🕮 Exploring Scripture

Psalm 138:8 says, "The LORD will perfect that which concerns me; Your mercy, O LORD, endures forever; do not forsake the works of Your hands."

According to this verse, who is responsible for perfecting your child? The LORD! You train, He perfects.

Ephesians 4:15–16 says, "Speaking the truth in love, may grow up in all things into Him who the head—Christ—from whom the whole body, joined and knit together by what every joint supplies, according to the effective working by which every part does its share, causes growth of the body for the edifying of itself in love." What does this say about each person's uniqueness?

For In-Depth Study

Read Jesus' parable about the sower in Luke 8:4–15. Verse 15 reads, "But the ones that fell on the good ground are those who, having heard the word with a noble and good heart, keep it and bear fruit with patience." Note that patience is required for bearing fruit. Nothing in life will help you to grow in patience as much as raising a child!

The Christian renewal and transformation process is life long. Romans 12:2 says, "And do not be conformed to this world, but be transformed by the renewing of your mind, that you may prove what is that good and acceptable and perfect will of God."

Is this transforming process always easy or sometimes painful?

📖 *Taking Action*

- In what ways have you nagged your wife or children? List something about which you've been too critical.

- How can you be more of an encourager? Write down something you really like about each of them. Is there something you already know they're working hard to change? Try to think of a specific way you can be an encourager.

Use this link to read more about or order Man in Command:

http://amzn.to/2ov4IHD

47385406R00124

Made in the USA
Middletown, DE
23 August 2017